OVERTHINKING

Discover How To Eliminate Negative Thinking, Overcome Fear, Anxiety, Stress & Declutter Your Mind. Learn How To Master Your Mind To Build Mental Toughness To Focus On The Present

Robert Cardone, New Thought Institute

© **Copyright 2022 - All rights reserved.**

The content contained within this book may not be reproduced, duplicated or transmitted without direct written permission from the author of the publisher.

Under no circumstances will any blame or legal responsability be held against the publisher, or author, for any damages, reparation, or monetary loss due to the information contained within this book, either directly or indirectly.

Legal Notice:

This book is copyright protected. It is only for personal use. You cannot amend, distribute, sell, use, quote or paraphrase any part, or the content within this book, without the consent of the author or publisher.

Disclaimer Notice:

Please note the information contained within this document is for educational and entertainment purposes only. All effort has been executed to present accurate, up to date, reliable, complete information. No warranties of any kind are declared or implied. Readers acknowledge that the author is and engaged in the rendering of legal, financial, medical or professional advice. The content within this book has been derived from various sources. Please consult a licensed professional before attempting any techniques outlined in this book.

By reading this document, the reader agrees that under no circumstances is the author responsible for any losses, direct or indirect, that are incurred as a result of the use of the information contained within this document, including, but not limited to, errors, omissions, or inaccuracies.

Download the Audiobook Version of This Book for FREE

and

GET a BONUS INSIDE

If you love listening to audio books on the go, I have great news for you. You can download the audio book version of this book for **FREE** just by signing up for **FREE** 30-day audible trial!

SCAN ME

Audible Trial Benefits

As an audible customer, you will receive the below benefits with your **30-day free trial**:

- **FREE** audible book copy of this book
- After the trial, you will get **1 credit** each month to use on any audiobook
- Your credits automatically roll over to the next month if you don't use them
- Choose from Audible's 200,000 + titles
- Listen anywhere with the **Audible app** across multiple devices
- Make easy, no-hassle exchanges of any audiobook you don't love
- Keep your audiobooks forever, even if you cancel your membership
- And much more

Table of contents

Introduction..6

What is negative thinking, and why does it exist?...14

The anxiety problem.....................................21

The anxiety solution.....................................35

Reducing worry with deusion........................45

Anxiety relapse and prevention.....................61

Stress and more problems............................66

Self-discipline why is so important...............75

Conclusion..90

INTRODUCTION

Overthinking is one of the main ills of our generation, and it is the culprit that makes us feel frustrated and tired. When we overthink, we go over our thoughts without concluding. What's more, sometimes we end up with ideas contradicting each other. We go, for example, from being excited about a date to questioning ourselves for hours and reviewing every detail of the meeting because we did something wrong. We begin to blame ourselves for scenarios that are not necessarily true. Medically, overthinking raises stress levels, reduces creativity, clouds judgment, and prevents you from making decisions. However, the good news is that there is a lot you can do about it. Here are seven steps to stop thinking. If you identify yourself as an overthinker and think of yourself as such, your brain will start overthinking because it thinks it's the right thing to do. Do not identify yourself as a person who overthinks and decides to identify as a decision-maker. You will see that you brainwash yourself – for good – by yourself over time. In the act of mindfulness, make a point of noticing whenever you are overthinking. Name the action and decree you will not give in. Focus on the moment. Or, write about what you feel. According to studies, writing helps metacognitive thinking, that is, awareness of your thoughts. This way, you will be able to understand why you feel the way you do, and you will be able to take action. It's not worth stressing about something you have no power over. Every time you catch yourself overthinking, ask yourself: can you do something about this situation? For example, think about what expenses you can cut or what income you can generate instead of getting overwhelmed by not having money to pay rent. Sometimes we overthink as a result of our irrational fears. Fear of being wrong, of what others think, of not being good enough, and we practically get into a very absurd drama because we suffer more in our minds than in reality. If you're scared, just step forward with your intentions and see what happens. You will see that it is not so serious. Also, the more you train yourself to act, the less you overthink.

To stop overthinking, it's time to change your way of thinking. Instead of throwing yourself into suffering, let off steam (return to the previous point of writing what overwhelms you), but just as you let go of your drama, think of solutions. Write the steps you could take. It also helps to get into the habit of mentioning possible solutions whenever you talk about your problems with someone.

People often blame and curse the environment and what happens around them because they identify it as the cause of their discomfort and suffering. But does the outside cause discomfort, or are your interpretations of what is happening around you what conditions your emotions?

Our thoughts influence our behaviors and our emotions. Depending on the psychological current or the professional you read or visit, you will label them negative, catastrophic, limiting, destructive or useless thoughts. What else gives the concept. What matters is their power to influence us, both positively and negatively.

Many patients say they have a head like a washing machine. Ideas, fears, terrifying speeches, and thoughts that do not stop spinning in my mind. They feel caught between worlds, unable to stop or ignore them. Some people hate relating to themselves because what "their mind tells them"Causes tremendous anguish.

There is two good news. The first: you are largely responsible for how you feel. It is not the environment that makes you anxious but your interpretation of the environment. This holds you accountable and allows you to control and act on your feelings. Many would like to disassociate themselves from everything and continue blaming society for their discomfort and how bad everything is. But this option limits you and leaves you without resources.

The second good news is that you can modify your cognitive style when you decide to train another way of thinking. Hundreds of thousands of people manage to prepare and finish a marathon despite how hard this test is. But when we talk about modifying what is related to the psyche, we immediately associate it with difficulty, a lack of willpower, and our way of being, and we question the possibility of change. Follow these tips to put thinking at bay.

Forget the idea of becoming a super positive and super optimistic person. The world is not pink, nor is it a black and hostile place. It is about seeking the usefulness of what you think. Thoughts and emotions are useful when they allow us to solve what worries us and useless when we can do nothing to relieve ourselves. Trust and delegate, and allow others to act autonomously in doing so. Excessive control generates anxiety. When delegating what you can't take responsibility for, imagine a switch in your mind and flip it off whenever worry arises. To stop paying attention to the useless is not irresponsible. On the contrary, allow it to be in the present.

How many times have you thought about the most empowering response you could have given in an argument... that happened five years ago? Or how many times have you thought that a relationship will not prosper because your crush looks like that ex you abandoned you, and they are the same? Overthinking is very much related to living in the past. And while it can't change, we can learn the lessons and make them work for us forever. Accept the past for what it was and free yourself from that burden. However, it is also common that suddenly, the thought attacks:

what time was today's meeting? You check the calendar, and there is nothing. The invitation didn't come in the mail, either. Could it be that they have not invited you? No, it can't be: the team always considers you to participate in the morning meetings.

This line of thinking is common. Overthinking the basic activities we have in the day happens. Even more so when it comes to situations that emotionally afflict us or are going through a rough patch. Thoughts settle inside us, and suddenly, it seems that we cannot let go of them: although it is not the healthiest thing mentally, we give them a thousand turns to find an answer that seems slightly acceptable to us. The problem begins when this type of mental wear manifests itself on a physical level or interferes with our relationships. Love breakups, difficult exams at school, strained relationships at work: any situation that represents an obstacle to our well-being is subject to these exhausting inner dynamics. The problem is that, generally, when the duel is so close, the mental image is distorted: it is out of focus. When people are flooded with negative thoughts, they are much more likely to suffer from anxiety ravages. In the most extreme cases, you can fall into a deep depression or have bouts of panic attacks. The most delicate thing about the matter is that the scenarios we create are often fictitious and far from what is happening in the world. To avoid falling into these obsessive patterns, it is important to identify what situations, stimuli, or attitudes trigger them. Some people are reactive when their loved ones talk dirty to them or the half-hearted responses they receive from their partners. Sometimes, all it takes is a message or post on social media to get the imagination flying over rough waters.

Thinking is a powerful human quality and tool for our survival. When we think about an issue, we are trying to find a useful solution in most cases. It works, mainly when it is, and it's about something we can have some control over.

However, we know it becomes counterproductive when we go from thinking to overthinking. Going round and round about a topic ceases to be something that works when it comes to situations where we cannot do anything directly. Trying to solve something out of our control by overthinking will only lead us to fears, doubts, uncertainties, terrible anticipations, bad forecasts, blockages, and painful emotions. Overthinking a lot can cause multiple problems and trigger other types of situations related to these that we will address in this book. However, its consequences: It can increase stress. As your sense of clarity and ability to solve problems are affected, this can increase the feeling of stress and lead you to experience some mental health problems. It can trigger anxiety and depression.

Blockages come from everywhere and occur at all points, and some are not malicious but are still obstacles that stop professional or personal activities. It is enough to have "the typical difficulties" for others caused by oneself to appear.

The good thing about challenges is that they serve to build a personal path. Achieving it is not easy, but it seems to be less burdensome for people with a clear mind. On the contrary, those who overthink everything make knots turn and stagnate, or it is very difficult for them to move forward.

Overthinking, like everything, has its good and bad sides. It prevents making dumb decisions or making dumb mistakes, but it also often stops when you want to make any decision or action.

The pressure that has been placed on you to make the right decisions is very great, so the urge to spend even more time thinking is very strong. It is believed that if you spend a lot of time thinking about a decision, you will eventually figure it out.

Well, thoughtful decisions are good and necessary, but in measure and not in excess. At a certain point, too much of something becomes a problem, and overthinking is for many.

Finding exactly when thinking becomes overthinking is complicated. But if you begin to doubt the decisions made more than twice, the ball of thread begins to roll.

OVERTHINKING

Overthinking is a habit that is not easily broken. So how do you begin to change the way you think? Practicing moving forward is powerful in mitigating the consequences of overthinking, such as anxiety and indecision. As we advance, don't allow thoughts to occupy your mind. fade and remain in the past. You have to learn from mistakes; they are life lessons, but they no longer have a current purpose. If you stay awake to mistakes, you will only reap doubts and more doubts.

All bad decisions are ghosts haunting future decisions. Personal weaknesses and failings should not govern actions. It's no use rethinking things because the past won't change any more. You will only feel anxiety, wishing that everything had been different.

The time invested in overthinking a past situation would be better used when a new opportunity presents itself so that the correct decisions can finally be made on that new occasion.

You can only think up to a certain point. Everything has limits. Decide something or take some action. Even if the expected results are not given, it is better than not doing something about it.

Feelings of worry take hold, and Fear, sadness, and hopelessness set in. Also, it can manifest with anger or irritability that eventually causes depression, and you will have a higher risk of experiencing an addiction. Affects the response of the immune system. Stressful situations cause hormones or substances like cortisol to be produced unnecessarily, harming your immune system. It can make you lose your creativity. When everything is calm in your brain and head, all cognitive and creative processes develop and happen more easily and naturally. It can increase your blood pressure and risk cardiovascular disease. The result of stress can increase your blood pressure and aggravate factors that increase the risk of heart disease, such as smoking, increased cholesterol levels, an unhealthy diet, etc. It will disturb your sleep. You will feel that your brain does not disconnect. This will alter your sleep pattern and its quality. It will be difficult for you to reconcile; therefore, you will have a non-refreshing sleep.

You can have changes at the digestive level. When you are stressed or thinking over and over again, digestive discomforts can appear that eventually cause irritable bowel syndrome, gastritis, or even ulcers in the digestive tract. It affects your memory. Overthinking unnecessarily puts your brain to work, affecting your cognitive ability and hampering your memory. Change your appetite. Stress can suppress or exaggerate your appetite through the secretion of certain hormones, affecting your usual food intake. It can paralyze you. To put it in some way, it can encourage non-action since you will feel unable to make decisions, solve problems, and take action and undertake.

However, many actions can be taken to improve overthinking. Be aware of these obsessive thoughts: You will know what you are facing. A good tip is to write these thoughts down, pause them and come back to them the next morning when we are calmer, and you can counteract them with positive and logical thoughts...Establish a time limit to make a difficult decision: When you let the mind enter that labyrinth of obsessive thoughts, it is losing the battle against yourself; Setting a time limit to organize and focus our thoughts is a good technique to make the best decision and not get caught in the loop of rumination. Change your focus of attention: It may sound like the simplest habit, but it is the hardest to do. Overthinking is getting on a treadmill that doesn't stop, but the one who has the control to get off that treadmill is yourself. Focusing on your breath can help you reduce your activation and return to the present moment. You can use meditation videos/audios or start by observing the movement of your breath in the body. See things from a broader perspective: It's all too easy to fall into the trap of overthinking and dissecting every stressful situation that comes our way. So when these obsessive thoughts kick in, try countering them with questions like Is this making me feel good? Is it bringing me joy? Will it be important in 4 years or four weeks? What consequences does overthinking bring me? These questions can quickly get you out of that state and help you let go of that situation. Focus your time and energy on the things that are important to you. Find something that brings you joy and satisfaction: Playing sports or activities that generate endorphins is a good strategy against excessive thinking. This hormone is responsible for reducing that feeling of discomfort and helps us focus on positive thoughts. Try the activities you like the most: running, walking, cycling, going out with friends, painting, etc.

That is why below, we will present you a guide that you can use to avoid these types of thoughts at all costs and thus manage to dominate your mind, avoiding anxiety problems, overthinking, and even irrational fears that this type of behavior can cause

WHAT IS NEGATIVE THINKING, AND WHY DOES IT EXIST?

Negative thoughts darken our lives and cause us a bad mood or pain. Getting rid of them from our minds can sometimes be difficult or very easy, depending on the current state of the people who suffer from them and their response to handling this type of situation. Our brain keeps all the information experienced throughout the day and saves it from processing it in the memory drawer. A day we have 50,000 thoughts, of which 10,000 are negative, and there are also times when certain thoughts can lead us to fall into the confusion of whether they are good or bad for us and if we do not know how to question them, they can do us a lot of harm.

When we start to have negative thoughts about the same subject, these can end up hurting us since they get bigger and bigger as we believe them more strongly.

The only thing negative thoughts do is take away our energy and take away all the strength and vitality we have from the moment we get up until we go to bed.

The more I believe my negative thoughts, the stronger they become, taking root in our thinking style, and it is much more difficult to avoid them.

Sometimes negative thoughts can hurt so much that they can

condition your life and character. In the end, these thoughts, if we do not know how to question them, can damage our way of valuing ourselves (self-esteem) or make us believe that innocuous situations or symptoms are a potential danger.

Negative thoughts haunt us and cloud our lives. However, they are ghosts that can be fought. There are several tangible reasons why these ideas appear in our minds. They are usually the result of various reasons that could easily be eliminated by taking a little awareness and wanting to improve our quality of life.

We are all human beings, which is why we sometimes have negative thoughts. Negative thoughts are ideas that make us weak, lose hope, or get in the way of improving our health. A negative thought is usually a criticism of oneself. Conceptually we can say that a negative thought is an image, idea, or phrase expressed mentally or verbally, which implicitly carries an unfavorable connotation of the context in which it occurs or the situation we would like to see ourselves. The striking thing about the case is that we are often unaware of their creation, so they emerge automatically. Our thoughts are part of our "mental map" that, together with the beliefs, values, rules, and the meaning that we attribute to the different experiences throughout life, constitute all those aspects that make us unique and different. And that determines our perception of the world and the environment in which we move.

It is known that the same experience or situation for some people can be interpreted as unpleasant and very stressful; others, on the other hand, may consider the same situation a challenge and the stress inherent in it as the engine to overcome it. Some well-known examples: are speaking in public, working in an emergency service, high-impact sports competitions, and risk sports ..... .among many others.

It can be said that the initial problem of this is when the first bad thoughts assail us, that if we do not know how to deal with them, they end up haunting our minds too much.

The typical phrase "don't think about it anymore and forget about it" is a mistake because the more we forget that thought that hurts us, the more present we have. In such a way, the idea hovers around us almost cyclically, continues in our heads, and can become an obsession.

Negative thoughts or unreasonable evaluations have often crossed our lives since we are constantly evaluating the situations that are going to be presented to us, but what we have to know is to value ourselves reasonably so that they do not affect us more than necessary and be aware that its content is neither objective. For this reason, we are going to know what the most common negative thoughts are that has surely crossed your mind at some time in your life:

The idea of believing that you know what others think: Sometimes we worry excessively about what others think of us, and in reality, it is impossible to know what others think about you, only that you think you know what they have in their head. This would be a cognitive distortion. Specifically, it is called mind reading.

Generalize situations: Falling into the generalization of events is one of the most frequent mistakes. You have to be more optimistic about life, and if something bad happens to you today, tomorrow will be another day, but the same thing will not happen to you every day.

Dramatize or play the victim: Making ourselves the victim in certain situations triggers negative thoughts, so we must try to avoid them so that they do not surface.

Insulting ourselves and those around us: We live these situations day in and day out, in such a way that we blame ourselves for the things that happen to us and underestimate ourselves and, in turn, make the people who are by our side also end up feeling bad.

Catastrophic or excessively exaggerated everyday events or symptoms: Faced with innocuous everyday events or symptoms, we transfer consequences terrible, generating great fears that, if not treated properly, will condition our lives.

Create unattainable expectations: It is very good to think that we can do everything and that we are capable of reaching the end of the world, but one thing must be clear, and that is that many times this can become a problem for ourselves because at Failure to meet these expectations can generate large doses of sadness or anxiety.

Taking away the value of positive things: This is another of the negative thoughts that can do us the most harm because if something good happens to us, we do not value it and continue to focus on the bad and dark things surrounding us.

Thinking that things are either white or black: We often do not stop to think that the things that happen to us or affect us are not always black or white; rather, there are greys. This generates a perfectionist style that can affect us a lot in the world of work or our day-to-day life. Seeing life from the extremes is not going to bring us anything good.

We can choose, act, and change our present and improve our future. Do we prefer to focus on the good or put all our attention on the negative?

What is "Fear," and why is it hard to face it?

Fear is a feeling of mistrust that leads to believing something negative will happen. It is the anguish in the face of a danger that, which is very important, can be real or imaginary. The relevance of this nuance is that although the danger does not exist because it is imaginary, Fear, on the contrary, can be very real.

Fear is an emotion that has an adaptive function since it prevents us from taking risks in situations in which we could get hurt. It helps us mobilize in the face of threatening or worrying circumstances so that we do what is necessary to avoid, assume or face the risk appropriately. The variety of stimuli that this emotion generates in us is so complete, so extensive that we can't enumerate them. Anything can cause Fear in a certain person.

Looking at it another way, when Fear becomes intense, it loses that function and turns into panic, a feeling of extreme Fear and sudden and overwhelming loss of control. You breathe rapidly and feel your heart pounding.

This can cause us to become paralyzed or act ineffectively in situations that are perceived as threatening. When we feel Fear, we believe we have a low capacity for control and prediction. However, we consider that we need to face it imminently, and to do so, we mobilize a whole series of behaviors. We always avoid and escape from what produces Fear in us. Fear paralyzes us and makes us focus all our attention on the triggering stimulus. In addition, it will facilitate defensive behaviors in those cases in which it is necessary. Other physiological reactions include increased cardiac pressure, sweating, dilated pupils, decreased body temperature, increased skin conductance, muscle tone, and even stiffening. In addition, there are times when the eliciting stimulus of this emotion generates a startle response in us when it occurs unexpectedly.

As we have seen, it is a very useful emotion when escaping from danger or potential danger. However, do not forget that it is also a barrier that prevents you from living life. If it is excessive: "Fear paralyzes us, blocks us emotionally, and makes it difficult for us to enjoy the small or great pleasures of life on many occasions."

Fear gives rise to a huge amount of psychological disorders. These include Obsessive-Compulsive Disorders, Anxiety Disorders, Panic Attacks, Post-Traumatic Stress Syndrome, and Phobias, which for something to be considered a phobia must have the following characteristics: Inevitably avoid the triggering stimulus or condition; The feeling of Fear is disproportionate compared to the real danger of it; We cannot control it; They produce a certain degree of restlessness and discomfort; There is no real justification for that sentiment.

Fear is a very useful emotion to escape or avoid danger. However, it is also a barrier that can get in the way of a person's enjoyment. If it is excessive, it can block and prevent the course of a normal life. . In fact, many of the most common disorders are caused by Fear of a real or possible situation, such as anxiety, phobias, or panic attacks.

The fear response is autonomous; we do not consciously activate it voluntarily. Experts establish four automatic responses: flight, aggressive defense, immobility, and submission. In addition, another physiological response occurs in which cardiac pressure increases, sweating while body temperature drops, pupils dilate and muscle tone increases, leading to stiffness.

Anything can scare a certain person, and it can be real Fear in the face of danger. It has an adaptive value or unreal if it has an imaginary, distorted and catastrophic origin, such as the Fear of flying or speaking in public. These are not adaptive fears since there is no real danger, and they can turn into phobias.

Thus, depending on their level, fears can be normal or pathological. The first are those that appear before harmful stimuli, have a short duration, and do not interfere with daily life. The pathological ones are the fears that are activated even when there is no danger and can last indefinitely in time.

There are different levels of Fear. There may be very mild fears, which appear as slight anguish, such as when there is going to be an exam, or a certain fear and anxiety when there is a problem. On the other extreme, Fear can reach a level of panic when we find ourselves in a situation where we perceive that our life is in danger.

We can think that Fear is excessive if it does not correspond to a dangerous situation. Also, we can assess how much this Fear affects us daily if it prevents us from doing certain things, if we don't know how to lose Fear or if we don't have the tools to handle it.

The current mentality about emotions is that, although some are more pleasant than others, they should not be conceived as "positive" and "negative." All of them are positive insofar as they are adaptive. Feeling them is always positive because they are useful to us, and we must feel them freely instead of repressing them or trying to control them. But, as with the rest of the emotions, Fear can become a problem, a symptom of a psychopathological process. Fear becomes problematic when our beliefs and interpretations cause us to feel it in an exaggerated and dysfunctional way, making what happens as a result of feeling that Fear much worse than what would happen if we did not feel it. That is, it does not help us but rather becomes something disadvantageous and maladaptive. If this happens, we will discuss a mental disorder or, at the very least, a psychological problem.

We have a context in which Fear is problematic as a symptom of many anxiety disorders, especially phobias. Although in some of them, what causes the pathological Fear has a certain meaning to be feared, the truth is that we speak of a phobia when the phobic reaction, the Fear, is more serious than the threat is supposed to be.

Fear is a fundamental emotion for our survival. We cannot live without Fear. Although we have been told the opposite, that Fear brings unhappiness. The truth is that our happiness and well-being depend a lot on it because not being afraid of things that could harm us is running the risk that they could affect us. Fear helps us avoid life's dangers, as long as it is a functional fear. If, on the other hand, Fear deprives us of opportunities and does us more harm than good, that is when we must remove it from our lives.

THE ANXIETY PROBLEM

Anxiety, like stress, is a body response to extreme situations, characterized by a feeling of mild anguish or Fear and the appearance of rapid heart rate and breathing, sweating, or a feeling of weakness. It is normal and can help me learn how to deal with complicated situations.

However, an anxiety crisis, without being a serious event for health, generates a panic situation that causes symptoms similar to those of a heart attack, to the point that it can be confused with it. It occurs instantaneously, without warning, reaches its maximum intensity in a few minutes, and can last for a few more.

Anxiety disorders occur in anxiety-prone personalities, people with normal personalities, and people with personality disorders. Generalized anxiety illnesses often begin concerning stressful events and become chronic when stressful events persist.

Anxiety disorders are abnormal states with physical and mental symptoms as a fundamental aspect and can be secondary to a psychiatric disorder or an organic disease.

The most frequent psychological symptoms are irritability, difficulty concentrating, hypersensitivity to noise, and an intense feeling of restlessness.

The person's appearance is characterized: his face looks tired, forehead wrinkled, tense posture, restless and often trembling, pale, sweaty, especially hands, feet, and armpits. Easy to cry and is appreciated more apprehensive than depressed.

Anxiety is one of the most common ailments in humans. It is described as a complex, diffuse and unpleasant emotion, expressed by a feeling of Fear and emotional tension accompanied by various bodily symptoms.

Anxiety is not Fear of anything because Fear is a feeling produced by a present, known, and imminent danger, and that is generally found alongside or linked to the objects or things that generate it, which differentiates anxiety from Fear, is that this is a sensation of a coming danger, indefinable, unpredictable, of vague and incomprehensible cause.

Anxiety is a normal emotion that has activating functions in the body's response to various stimuli, thus facilitating the individual's ability to respond. But... when the anxiety is exceeded in intensity, frequency, or duration. Or it appears associated with stimuli that, without representing a real threat to the body, produce serious emotional and functional alterations, then it is considered a disease situation.

Anxiety is confused with anguish, although both are very similar reactions in reality. Relevant detail is that in anguish, physical symptoms predominate in people: the almost theatrical anxious situation, more pain in the heart, in the precordial region or throat, pressure in the stomach, and feeling of suffocation.

Anxiety is generally associated with depression, so care should be taken with severely agitated depressives and generalized anxiety.

Anxiety is a natural adaptive mechanism that allows us to be alert to compromised events. A certain degree of anxiety provides an adequate component of precaution in especially dangerous situations. Moderate anxiety can help us stay focused and face the challenges ahead.

Sometimes, however, the anxiety response system is overwhelmed and malfunctions. More specifically, anxiety is disproportionate to the situation and sometimes even occurs without obvious danger. The subject feels paralyzed with a feeling of helplessness and, in general, a deterioration of psychosocial and physiological functioning. It is said that when anxiety occurs at inappropriate times or is so intense and long-lasting that it interferes with the person's normal activities, it is considered a disorder.

Anxiety disorders are, as a whole, the most frequent psychiatric illness, this being because it manifests themselves in many ways and especially in those people who usually have problems with self-confidence about any area that surrounds them in their general life, as well as in people who tend to overthink things or overthink the slightest fact that has happened to them an instant ago.

Anxiety disorders usually worsen these types of situations, thanks to the fact that they can manifest themselves in the following ways:

- Phobias: Phobia is a disproportionate fear concerning some real danger. If a phobia interferes with the ability to lead a normal life, it may be considered an anxiety disorder. Common phobias are Fear of heights, spiders, rats, blood, injections, or enclosed spaces.

- Panic disorder: A person with panic disorder may suddenly experience periods of intense Fear, known as panic attacks. Panic attacks may be triggered by something, and they may happen for no apparent reason. Panic attacks usually last 5-10 minutes but can last longer.

- Obsessive-compulsive disorder: A person with obsessive-compulsive disorder (OCD) may experience frequent obsessions and compulsions that cause anxiety. Symptoms of OCD range from mild to severe, including obsessions (recurring thoughts that cause distress or anxiety) and compulsions (actions or rituals deemed necessary to counteract the obsessions).

- Post-traumatic stress disorder: Post-traumatic stress disorder (PTSD) can develop after experiencing or witnessing a traumatic event. PTSD symptoms include anxiety, which can come and go, and recurrent thoughts, memories, images, dreams, or distressing flashbacks of the traumatic event. PTSD can develop many years after the traumatic event.

•   Generalized Anxiety Disorder: Anxiety can be a chronic disorder in which you worry most of the time about things that might go wrong. This is called generalized anxiety disorder (GAD). If you have GAD, you may also have panic attacks and some phobias.

But one can come to ask how is it that this type of situation arose in my life? Well, the truth is that there can be many. Anxiety can have many causes, and it may not be clear why you have anxiety. Still, you are more likely to have an anxiety disorder if: you are experiencing a stressful and critical situation, such as the loss of a loved one, or experience a traumatic event, have another mental health problem, for example, depression or alcohol dependence, have a physical illness, such as a thyroid disorder, or use illegal substances, for example, amphetamines, LSD, and ecstasy, or even after long-term use of any medicine, such as a tranquilizer, you are stopping taking it. Some people are born with a tendency to be more anxious than others, which means that anxiety disorders could be due to genetic inheritance. Similarly, people who are not naturally anxious may become so if they are put under intense pressure.

the Alarm Response

The group of changes that occur in the body to help a person fight or flee from stressful or dangerous situations. It is the body's way of helping to protect itself from harm. Certain hormones, such as adrenaline and cortisol, are released into the blood during fight or flight, and this causes an increase in blood pressure, heart rate, and breathing. Other changes are increased blood sugar, wakefulness, muscle tension, and sweating. It is characterized by the release of ACTH by the pituitary gland and adrenaline by the medulla of the adrenal gland, which translates into an increase in blood glucose and faster breathing that increases the level of oxygen in the blood; These actions manage to provide the body with more energy to face the stressful situation. These reactions are only part of how the body responds to imminent danger in three phases: alarm, adaptation, and exhaustion.

ALARM PHASE:

It is a means of defense against an immediate and real threat. The body responds without being aware of it and prepares us to avoid the risk or face it with all available energy. The neuroendocrine system is responsible for the immediate reaction through the secretion of hormones that accelerate the pulse, increase the respiratory rate, and make us more excitable so that our reaction can occur quickly. The body prepares at breakneck speed for fight or flight, and internal changes will occur that will reduce losses in either case. The fight or flight will burn the energies; the body will normally recover from this effort if all goes well.

Adrenaline and noradrenaline activate all the systems to work to the limit, adapting to the needs of a short space of time; the secreted cortisol collaborates in the recovery action, providing energy and producing anti-inflammatory effects.

The drawback is that such a powerful reaction, repeated many times by minor stressors, requires the body to submit to a forced load that is not without risk; adrenaline consumes us, and cortisone attacks the immune system when we react excessively to any stressor.

This is the immediate response to a job threat or challenge. The mobilization of the autonomic nervous system provokes a stress response. The body systems coordinate preparation for action, affecting mood, regulating the cardiovascular system, respiration, muscle tension, and motor activities.

The symptoms of this phase can be: palpitations, rapid breathing, wheezing, muscle tension (especially in the back, neck, and shoulders), dry throat, nausea, and anxiety.

RESISTANCE PHASE

When the alarm phase is repeated or is maintained over time, the body reacts by adapting to the effort required, whether it is the height of living in a flat with noisy neighbors; if nothing can be done to return to the original organic balance, the body will adapt, if possible, although paying a cost, a surcharge on the price of existence, this surcharge is paid for having taken the body out of the homeostatic balance in which it was so comfortable, the body continues to function but not as fine as before. We can imagine a car that always carries a 50 kg bag as an extra will continue to work. It adapts, its systems adapt to the new effort, its mechanics suffer a little more, its engine suffers a little more, its air resistance is more deficient, etc., will not be able to compete with other cars in its category without being overweight. It will probably last less too.

In the human body, the systems are much more intimately connected than in a car; many are going to be the side effects of a repeated alarm phase since, in addition to affecting the ergonomic and energetic functioning of the human vehicle, the same way of perceiving the life will be modified, new limitations are added to previous ones. The worst thing is that even this can happen so slowly that we hardly notice it or even consider it normal; I don't notice the effort since the autonomic nervous system does everything independently. I can notice the effects:

• Occasional headaches, which recur little by little more often

• A chronic fatigue that does not seem to go away with rest if it did.

• Circulatory problems, heaviness in the legs, varicose veins, perhaps.

• Muscle contractures in the neck, back, and lower back do not go away when resting. • Occasional loss of memory, which increases and irritates me at first. • Stomach aches, digestion problems, constipation. • Nervous tics. • sleep difficulty, or rest.• Increase in addictions, food, drink, and tobacco.· Lack of concentration.· Pessimism.· Feeling of Failure

The alarm reaction cannot be sustained indefinitely, and longer exposure to stressors leads to reaching the resistance phase. In this phase, a survival strategy is developed and a way of coping with the situation that the stressor has initiated. The reaction mechanisms can be both adequate and inappropriate.

People prefer short-term mitigation of their problems to long-term solutions and try to escape unfavorable situations with a quick fix. But it is necessary to identify measures that can lead not to this immediate "patchwork" but

long-term benefit.

The Exhaustion Phase.

There comes a time when the body cannot continue the effort. After continuous resistance, the energies run out.

The internal balance is broken after being threatened for a long time, and the immune system is affected, the ability to resist pathogens of any type decreases, and the disease appears; if the previous wear has been enough, even life is in danger, otherwise the body after sufficient rest still partially recovers although with sequelae derived from the collapse suffered; strokes, hypertension, ulcers, heart attack, cancer, infections, have the door open in a weakened organism.

When the demands placed on the body and mind are too high or cannot be met appropriately, the person "burns out." Prolonged stress leads to chronic problems, and the depletion of all reserves and energy can be the trigger for generalized depression.

In turn, the symptoms of the exhaustion phase can be divided into three aspects: physical, emotional, and mental:

Physical disorders. Headaches caused by tension, migraines, irritable bowel syndrome, decreased resistance to illnesses (colds and other "viral" ailments), exacerbation of asthma, dermatitis, psoriasis, back pain, gastritis, high blood pressure...

These symptoms are usually accompanied by a general feeling of tiredness, lack of energy, and weakness. Sleep habits tend to be modified, and weight gain or loss caused by changes in eating habits is common. In the workplace, those affected by this phase try to hide their symptoms until they overwhelm them and become uncontrollable.

Emotional disorders. The most frequent are depression, anxiety syndrome, and even suicidal ideas. These disorders manifest as uncontrolled anger, lack of interest in friends, hobbies, or family, and indifference to personal aspects such as exercise, clothing, and diet. The development of this phase leads to a decrease in performance, a loss of self-esteem, and a negative attitude towards work.

Symptoms of mental dysfunction- They can be accidents or near-accidents, difficulty concentrating, constant delays, absenteeism, increased errors and excuses, or sudden loss of memory of things close in time.

Assessment. As one walks through life, one tends to present certain behaviors or actions that are safe for each person. This generally arises as a security mechanism in the form of a wire wall that surrounds us and protects us from situations that would not normally be dangerous. Still, under the consideration of each one, it is. When we experience Fear or danger, we instinctively act quickly to avoid this type of danger, such as running long distances or even doing things we had never been encouraged to do before to feel safe.

If you find yourself in a dark parking lot with no visible lights and out of nowhere you hear a series of dry footsteps behind you, your first reaction is most likely to be to run directly towards your car for your safety or even turn around. To see first and then run to the car to ensure the possibly dangerous situation we find ourselves in. In addition, what is done would be to seek security in response to the physical problem or the threatening situation in which he finds himself. He will also seek security to relieve the episode of anxiety arising from the situation when he worries about something, be it dangerous or not.. These types of safety behaviors are actions that we and our bodies choose as a response that is carried out for our protection from emotions such as Fear and anxiety and from the disasters that these could cause or from disasters that worry us.

These safety behaviors are compelling as they immediately provide us with immediate benefits, such as reducing the sense of danger immediately or in the short term during the event. For example, if you suffer from OCD, an invitation to go out to dinner may trigger you to worry about exposing yourself directly to germs in the places where you sit or touch, including crowds of people around you, bacteria that could contain the food served to you and germs in public restrooms. On the other hand, if you reject this situation, avoiding first-hand going to the restaurant and all the possible fears mentioned above that are attributed to it, you will immediately feel relief. If you decide to go, you would need to take a whole series and list of precautions (safety behaviors) to avoid this type of danger, such as bringing antibacterial wipes, wearing bathroom door gloves, and eating only salad.

These securities or behaviors help us relieve anxiety in a certain way. Still, they can also worsen our situation since they may relieve us of the problems at that moment. Still, in the long run, it will generate a much greater difficulty since the Fear of diseases and bacteria will remain and could get worse because no precise action has been taken.

These behaviors are called safety behaviors, mainly of avoiding situations and approaching them. With avoidant security, some behaviors avoid, delay, or cause you to flee from Fear. This adaptive behavior is very attractive because it consists of nothing more than walking away from the problem and because you get an immediate decrease in your level of anxiety. With approach security, other behaviors are presented, where you get involved in situations that cause you anxiety. However, strategies are followed to prevent or minimize the results that are often feared. Both cause relief and make you feel better, but their differences are understandable. However, the problem with this behavior is that you never learn anything with certainty. Since you do not learn if the situation or experience you are experiencing will cause us tangible harm, you will never learn to tolerate the uncertainty of what could happen. Happen in the situation, and above all, you do not learn to trust your judgment in the situations you experience. So the next time you go through any of these situations, the same threat will appear, and you will experience the same anxiety, so you will decide whether to ward it off with the same security behavior or a new one. You live in a recursive loop where anxiety tends to become more frequent and intense, no less.

However, these two types of safety behaviors are not unique. Still, other types may not be as common, but that can also occur and perhaps allow learning from this type of situation, especially in those that make us very anxious. Verifying that everything has been done correctly or that you have carried out a certain activity or verifying it again is a safety behavior since it makes you feel less anxious when you do not remember if you did it or when faced with uncertainty. Another type of behavior is to overprepare yourself for any situation, whether by reading, informing yourself, or researching what you are going to do; this will allow us to have plenty of information and prepare ourselves as much as possible to reduce risk scenarios and reduce the uncertainty of facing a situation that causes us anxiety and can be a challenge for us. There is also perfectionism, whose goal is to eliminate any uncertainty that we have or any possibility of error when doing anything; this also implies that anyone cannot help us since this would imply that they do things differently. Also means that you have to work extra to avoid any errors. This also includes traditions or rituals that we regularly have so that they give us luck or even rituals in a certain religious way that implies greater self-security, such as a small dance to the fact of making a prayer for someone we love and something bad does not happen to him or so that similar things do not happen to us. It may also be that you carry specific objects that give you this security, such as a lucky charm, memories of someone, or even photos that give you this security of your own.

All these behaviors will allow you to evaluate the level of stress that you are suffering in the different situations in which it can manifest itself. Now you will be able to know certain safety behaviors that will help you measure the degree of fear or anxiety that is experienced and how we can eliminate it directly and even learn or not for future cases that are presented to us.

Motivation

Our brain is designed to focus on negativity rather than the positive, uncertainty rather than certainty. For some reason, news that carries some morbidity will be easier to arouse our curiosity, such as an accident, a disaster, etc., although later we repair and modify our thinking. Anxiety feeds easily on sensational, negative, and speculative news, so, at this time, it becomes more pertinent to control that diet or bombardment of information. Therefore, we must make a personal filter of what we want to feed our minds. It is also important to identify how impressionable our mind is, to which thoughts we give more space and those which are useful to us, which are overwhelming us, and then direct attention to things you have good control. It's been shown that when we shift our focus to what we can control, we see encouraging, significant, and lasting differences in our well-being and emotional health, remembering that some overwhelming thoughts or worries can't be avoided. Still, we can start by controlling the response to them. It's been shown that people who experience anxiety have a low tolerance for uncertainty. However, uncertainty is an inevitable and necessary part of our lives, and the more we manage and adapt to it, the sooner we can reduce mental distress. The ideal is, therefore, the acceptance that uncertainty and change are part of life; meditation is one option to achieve this. Another option is thought challenge, a technique that uses cognitive behavioral therapy with good results and is based on some of the following questions: when worrying or catastrophic thoughts occur, pause and ask yourself, what is my mind telling me? ?; do not believe all your thoughts, veil them and repeat, "they are just thoughts," remembering that you are not your thoughts; they are part of you. However, many times it seems that we lack motivation to do things; maintaining a structure and habits generates greater mental well-being, and for this, routines help increase our security and minimize feelings of overwhelm

For this, we must find motivation in the daily situations that we live in and do not usually look for it since this will relieve anxiety and distract us with other types of things that we are not normally used to doing, helping us overthink things. Schedule regular breaks after a certain time in front of the computer, after working at home, or in the office. For this, it is necessary that you give yourself some time to enjoy your life fully and what you are doing without feeling the need to rush, which implies that you either take a bath or prepare a coffee as you like, but what matters is that you do it consciously of what you are doing and that it is directly for your benefit. Take a walk, and appreciate how beautiful life is around you. Another way to motivate yourself is to write down and list weekly goals that benefit you. This will allow you to divide the responsibility into small activities throughout the week and prevent anxiety from recurring every day for things that you have not yet done or had not contemplated. You can also identify the most important and urgent tasks you have to perform and the secondary ones, ensuring that the first ones are a priority and the secondary ones take a backseat, avoiding stressing about it. Prepare the to-do list that you will have the next day as a way of planning, taking into account any unforeseen event so that situations do not arise that you did not plan and could cause fear or anxiety. You can also order your space at the end of the day, ensuring that everything is left as it was in its original position and an orderly manner before the night and also when you finish occupying it, so that the next morning you do not have to waste time and generate that feeling of anxiety when seeing everything messy. Decide on a regular sleep schedule. Create a ritual to end the work activity. It can be put on comfortable clothes, close the computer and any work device, or put on music. Be kind to yourself, you may not always follow through, and you may as well try again. Practice gratitude daily, both on a spiritual level and among people, thoroughly enjoy small and big things, enjoy the small pleasant moments, enjoy and be grateful for your bed, a good talk, a sincere message and be thankful for everything. Begin with a daily deep breathing practice. Start by training your breathing and be patient because you will do better each day. Start by practicing abdominal breathing: placing one hand on your chest and the other on your stomach, inhale gently and slowly counting one, two, three, while noticing how to expand your stomach, hold your breath again for a count of one, two, three slowly exhale through your mouth for a slow count of one, two, three, do this for five to ten minutes at least twice a day. Initiate or enhance social relationships

It is also possible that Look for a volunteer community line by phone. Schedule live chat meetings with friends promoting positive topics such as a book or movie to comment on, have a list of friends, friends, and family that you call periodically, and try a short but pleasant talk, send written letters.

Exercise is also very important. Whether inside your home or outside, whether aerobic or non-aerobic exercise, the importance of exercise will be reflected in constant activation, reducing anxious thoughts, and improving your response to stress; it is important to find something that you enjoy when it comes to acquiring a habit of exercise, nowadays physical conditioning has acquired an importance not only in health but also socially and there are many tools to do it at home, activities can be searched online, videos of (practically) any existing activity. Studies suggest that with 20 minutes three times a week, you begin to experience its benefits. Depending on the individual circumstances and health conditions of the moment, some physical activity options may be: schedule a daily walk, complete a series of activities online, or invest in some training equipment as long as you have already verified that it will be useful you.

THE ANXIETY SOLUTION

We all feel anxiety and stress from time to time. Some situations often trigger anxiety, such as meeting tight deadlines, important social obligations, or driving in heavy traffic. This mild anxiety can help keep you alert and focused to deal with threatening or difficult situations.

But people who experience extreme Fear and lingering worry may be dealing with anxiety disorders. The frequency and intensity of this type of anxiety is often debilitating and interferes with daily activities. However, with proper and effective treatment, people with anxiety disorders can lead normal lives.

There are several main types of anxiety disorders. Each has its characteristics People with generalized anxiety disorders have recurring fears or worries, such as health or finances, and often have a constant feeling that something bad is about to happen. The cause of these intense feelings of anxiety can be difficult to identify. However, fears and worries are real and often prevent people from concentrating on their daily tasks. Panic disorder involves sudden, intense, and unprovoked feelings of terror and dread. Typically, people with this disorder become very fearful about when and how their next panic attack will strike, often limiting their activities. A related disorder includes phobias, or intense fears, about certain objects or situations. Specific phobias can include situations such as meeting certain animals or flying on an airplane, while social phobias include Fear related to social settings or public places. Obsessive-compulsive disorder is characterized by persistent, uncontrollable, and unwanted thoughts or feelings (obsessions) and routines or rituals people do to try to avoid or free themselves from these thoughts (compulsions). Examples of common compulsions include excessive handwashing or housecleaning for Fear of germs, or checking something over and over again for errors. Some people with severe physical or emotional trauma, such as from a natural disaster, serious accident, or crime, can experience post-traumatic stress disorder. Thoughts, feelings, and behavior patterns are seriously affected by memories of these events, sometimes for months or even years after the traumatic experience.

Symptoms such as extreme Fear, shortness of breath, rapid heart rate, insomnia, nausea , tremors, and dizziness are common in these anxiety disorders. Although they can occur anytime, anxiety disorders often emerge in adolescence or early adulthood. There is some evidence that anxiety disorders run in families. Genes and early learning experiences in families make some people more likely than others to have these disorders.

If left untreated, anxiety disorders can have serious consequences. For example, some people with recurring panic attacks strongly avoid putting themselves in situations they fear might trigger an attack. This avoidance behavior can create problems if it conflicts with job requirements, family obligations, or other basic activities of daily living.

Many people with untreated anxiety disorders are prone to other psychological disorders, such as depression, and have an increased tendency to abuse alcohol and other drugs. Your relationships with family, friends, and co-workers can become strained, and your job performance may decline.

Anxiety, that horrible feeling that comes on during and after a particularly hard day. It often appears for no reason and does not have a specific cause, as we have already observed. Normally, it is associated with work stress or what psychologists call "empacho de futuro", to the detriment of melancholy, which would be "pacho of the past". This disease is so common that legal recognition of this pathology is already demanded to receive compensation for labor damages and prejudice.

Cognitive-behavioral therapy includes a wide variety of techniques. One of them is the so-called "exposure therapy "; It challenges the person to vividly imagine the typical fear situation preceding the anxiety attack. The objective is to gradually and always with the help of a therapist submit to the risk situations that produce anxiety in real life to modify the irrational fear response. Another is learning cognitive techniques to change thought patterns leading to anxiety. This type of therapy is believed to be more effective than others,

When a person is diagnosed with anxiety by a medical professional, the first treatment is the classic antidepressants. Some studies indicate they can reduce symptoms in 60 to 70% of cases. Because they are highly criticized and usually do not solve the problem but put a chemical remedy in the short term, other types of drugs can be taken, such as beta-blockers, aimed at treating heart problems and high blood pressure, and anticholinergics to reduce specific symptoms, such as hand tremors or sweating. Antidepressants can have adverse side effects including nausea, sexual dysfunction, and hypertension. The alternative is often benzodiazepines, which can quickly relieve and control anxiety, but are extremely addictive when taken long-term.

Caffeine is a psychostimulant and there is a lot of research to suggest that it can exacerbate the symptoms of Generalized Anxiety Disorder (GAD) and trigger panic attacks.

In the same way, it is not advisable to resort to alcohol and its sedative properties . This can create a vicious cycle, where stress levels rise once the alcohol is processed and the initial effects wear off.

However, other much more casual ways will allow you to beat anxiety episodes and reduce it.

Anxiety is often triggered by daily stress and improvisation in the face of events. It is important to keep a schedule, plan appointments and spend a few minutes each morning drawing up our action plan. The daily rhythm of life allows us to have just enough time to dedicate ourselves solely to obligations. However, it is important to return to ourselves, dedicate time to what we feel like doing, with or without company. It allows you to relax, disconnect and restart. Relaxation techniques, such as diaphragmatic breathing, mindfulness, yoga or meditation can help us know how to better channel our thoughts. Once we calm down physically and mentally, we will know how to act better on a day-to-day basis and that anxiety that we usually feel will not appear.

When we allow ourselves to be influenced by fashion in sports activities, we can practice a sport that we will not always get the most out of. Sport should relax us, give us energy, motivate and de-stress. If what we are doing does not achieve it or reaches higher mental activation, we must look for another. Within this you can find yoga, massage therapies or meditation are activities that can help keep anxiety at bay. Try them. Similarly, practicing relaxation techniques for 30 minutes two or three times a day can mitigate the bad effects of muscle tension, one of the possible sources of anxiety.

It is also possible that you seek help in combating your thoughts. Fortunately, we can change these thoughts, and the first step is identifying them.

Negative thoughts usually come in the form of "what if," "all or nothing" thinking, or "excessive catastrophizing," such as, "What if I don't pass this test?" or "What if the plane crashes?", "What if I make a fool of myself?"

It is important to ask yourself : "Is this concern realistic?" "Is it really likely to happen?" "If the worst possible outcome happens, what would be so bad?", "Can I do it?", "What could I do?", "If something bad happens, what could it mean for me? "," "Is this true or does it just seem that way to me? What could I do to prepare myself for what might happen?

So, reframe or correct what you think would be more accurate, realistic, and adaptable. Conductance Biofeedback can help you control your anxiety and work on eliminating obsessive or recurring thoughts.

Avoid caffeine consumption, as Anxiety Management is as much about what you do as it is about what you don't do. And some substances exacerbate anxiety. Caffeine is one of those substances. This includes addictive substances, since while drugs and alcohol can help reduce anxiety in the short term, they often do the opposite in the long term. Even the short-term effect can be detrimental to anxiety. It is not the solution to your problems.

Learn relaxation techniques. Currently there are many ways to achieve the desired emotional and physical deactivation. We recommend Biofeedback for its objectivity and speed. Still, you can combine this Method and its initial phases based on physiological deactivation with the most effective stress and anxiety control techniques. That's what we offer at Nastia , again we insist on our goal: Help you regain control.

Acceptance of anxiety does not mean giving up on getting better and living a life of continual anxiety-affected moods. It simply means living with certain unpleasant emotional states that are unavoidable, but that we must make transitory.

Choose what you eat and how you eat it, since certain foods can harm you, such as coffee by activating you. But some foods can also make you bloated or uncomfortable, predisposing you to be more alert. To combat anxiety and prevent it, we must anchor our lives to the present , the skills we have or the things that bring us well-being. From there, together with small habits that should not be neglected, we will learn to be calm and have a lower average activation level.

You Can Face afraid

As we have already seen, Fear is a primary emotion that alerts us to a possible threat and indicates that we must take measures to protect ourselves. Therefore, its main objective is to keep us safe, the problem comes when it is Fear itself that does not let us live. However, Living without Fear is not possible, Fear is necessary, but overcoming the Fear that prevents us from moving forward, the one that blocks us, is one of the best ways to grow as people and to achieve a fuller life. This implies that we are not only afraid when we perceive a real threat to our "physical self" but also when we imagine a situation that could represent a danger . Our ability to anticipate danger allows us to take action to avoid it and keep ourselves safe, so these are perfectly understandable and rational fears. We can also feel Fear when we remember an event from the past, even if there is not the remotest possibility that it will happen again . The root of this Fear is normally entrenched in our unconscious and is very difficult to eliminate, since it can be activated even by a verbal allusion. To overcome this Fear, it is essential to work with techniques such as hypnosis or EMDR , which allow us to access the negative memories of the past recorded in our brain and free ourselves from their emotional burden.

But perhaps the most incapacitating Fear is the one suffered by people who have a panic disorder, we would speak here of Fear in capital letters, since Fear is given a twist: the Fear of being afraid .

Throughout our lives we face different situations full of uncertainty that cause us Fear. This is how we develop Fear of Failure, Fear of rejection, Fear of loss, Fear of death and, above all, big changes.

These fears become a barrier that prevents us from living fully. Fear forces us to stay in our comfort zone and does not allow us to move forward and develop, it limits our goals and our actions, it keeps us blocked.

Of course, this type of Fear acts surreptitiously, generating doubts, sometimes obsessive, making us focus on the negative aspects of our performance or affecting our self-esteem.

In this way, Fear paralyzes us by sabotaging us and turning us into insecure people who abandon their projects long before they start. In these cases, Fear ceases to be a warning mechanism against possible dangers and becomes an attitude towards life that biases our growth.

Although we cannot (nor should we) eliminate Fear from our lives, we can learn to live with it, manage it, and prevent it from blocking our lives or paralyzing us.

When it comes to an irrational fear, the first step is to understand that your reaction is completely disproportionate and that there is no logical basis for that Fear, in this sense, cognitive behavioral therapy is very useful.

It is also important that you learn to accept Fear instead of fighting it. Your fears are a reaction to something you think is threatening, and it is normal for you to feel scared, the more you try to fight this feeling, the stronger it will be. Overcoming Fear involves knowing exactly what causes you to fear and being aware of your emotional and physiological reactions. A very useful tool in this regard is mindfulness.

The next step is to not let Fear paralyze you, to face it . A proverb says "Fear knocked on my door and when I opened it there was no one there. "Keep going despite the Fear, look to the future and look for new strategies or different alternatives that allow you to achieve the goal you have set for yourself. Develop confidence in your abilities and realize that the worst possible scenario is often not as dire as you imagine. Never, but never should you let Fear paralyze you, on the contrary, you should take enough strength to face it. Even if you are afraid, you must be a brave girl or boy to achieve your goals, trusting in your abilities. And understanding that not all situations are involved in dire scenarios.

Stop running away. When you are afraid of something, it is natural to make excuses to avoid facing it. However, this reaction causes even more Fear as it chases you with more force. With this attitude of flight you end up being afraid of Fear, which is much worse. Running away is not a good idea because what you fear will not go away unless you look at it, reflect on it and discover the best solution to face it.

Stop denying them. Many people find it difficult to accept that they are afraid, and they deceive themselves by telling false stories to show a courage they do not have. The first step in overcoming Fear is accepting it. If you do not accept that you have a certain fear, you will hardly be able to put an end to it. Well, you need to know how to look at yourself, observe what is happening to you and admit it. Without this step, you will not be able to move forward.

Stop fighting. Don't see Fear as an enemy you have to defeat because it will always beat you. The more you fight, the bigger and more powerful he becomes . Realize that deep down it is a fight with yourself.

Make friends with your fears. Allow yourself to feel the Fear in your body. Observe it and identify how it manifests itself, in which parts of your body, how you react, do your hands sweat? Does your heart race? Does your voice tremble? Do you blush? happens to you when you feel Fear? When you have it well-identified and realize that it is just a bodily sensation, you will not die from it and will begin to be able to face it. It is about normalizing it as a simple uncomfortable and passing emotion.

Treat them as an opportunity to grow. It doesn't matter how afraid you are that anxiety will make an appearance or that you will start to get very nervous. You have to overcome that Fear and for that you have to feel it. Once you are in the situation, think about why you have that Fear, is something really bad going to happen to you? Are you in real danger? Change your perspective and see fears as great teachers that challenge you to go beyond yourself. Do what scares you. It's the only way you have to finally get rid of him.

Another technique to deal with Fear or anxiety is live exposure, which consists of doing real rehearsals, in reality, and not just in imagination. This could be exposing yourself to that job interview that scared you so much, or exposing yourself to the feared situations that you suffer in your life, either while you are relaxed and expose yourself directly or once you psych yourself up and expose yourself to fear. .

Often, and especially today, Fear usually comes from a completely irrational fact. In this way, one way to control Fear is precisely by seeing where these feelings of Fear come from. Just because you're afraid of a situation doesn't mean you can't do anything about it.

Overcoming a fear is difficult, and this is why you must find some method with which you can motivate yourself to fight the Fear you have. The positive self-talk technique can be ideal for turning negative thoughts into positive ones. When you have this self-motivation , it will surely be easier to face your fears.

One of the most effective options to lose Fear is to visualize that you can face it. In this way, you can change the perspective of a situation and see another point of view with which you can control Fear.

In all types of fears , one of the parts that most influences their development are precisely the thoughts. In this way, in most cases, if we become aware of what is happening inside us, we can overcome Fear.

To control Fear you must know why you feel these fears. In this way, every time you have a panic attack or you see yourself conquered by Fear, you should try to analyze where it comes from. This is how you will be able to discover what is the cause of the fears that persecute you and you will be able to solve it. To learn to live without Fear, it is important to know how to analyze our internal thoughts, listen to them and change your internal language to be more positive. As you learn to challenge your negative thoughts and replace them with healthier ones, you will find that you will be able to overcome your fears and insecurities. While distracting yourself won't do you any good, it can be useful when you have your daily fears analyzed. Anything to take your mind off what you've been fearing can help recharge your strength to face the Fear that paralyzes you.

Rest assured it will be a long process that will require some effort. First, the only way to overcome Fear is to face it. That is, when you are in a moment that is not to your liking, and you want to run away from it because you do not want to face it, the best thing you can do is act and not get carried away by your instincts. And to achieve this, think coldly about the situation in which you find yourself and then decide what pros and cons it can bring you to what you are facing.

REDUCING WORRY WITH DEUSION

If we try to think about who we are, it may be difficult for us to realize that we are someone different from the little voice in our head that does not stop talking. We are very used to recognizing ourselves in our words and our thoughts. Most thoughts are automatically generated by our mind, perhaps as a reaction to certain stimuli or because we have remembered something we experienced in the past. The important thing is that we rarely create a thought voluntarily of everything we think.

This would not be a problem if we did not pay much attention to these thoughts. We sometimes believe that because a certain thought has crossed our minds, we are bad people, we are not capable of carrying out this or that activity, or even that we are crazy.

If you are one of those who listen too much to that inner voice that tells you how it is and how it is not, perhaps you are too fused with your thoughts.

Cognitive fusion causes the person to not distinguish between the thought and the conditions that produce that thought. That is, the person tends to believe the thought as absolute truth and forgets to contrast it with the reality that has caused it. Suddenly it is as if we have merged with our minds and cannot take perspective. Through cognitive defusion, the patient is expected to understand or know how to differentiate that their thoughts are just thoughts and not definite facts of reality.

By establishing that the negative and intrusive thoughts that the patient is presenting are not real facts, they would tend to lose their importance in terms of the discomfort they generate.

Cognitive defusion aims to build an experience similar to what children learn about dreams.

When we say "it was just a dream," it does not imply that this was not uncomfortable or even painful, only that we should not as if it were a reality.

Intrusive thoughts are those ideas that we have stuck in our minds. When these thoughts become recurrent, they can cause anguish and discomfort.

According to the cognitive diffusion approach, the affected person doesn't need to change their thinking; what is decisive is that they understand that thinking in a certain way does not explicitly influence their reality, as long as they do not lead that thought to the action.

Cognitive defusion techniques propose maintaining the thoughts that the person has and are only in charge of undoing the fusion between those thoughts and the symptomatology that the patient presents.

During the process of cognitive diffusion, the individual should start to see their unwanted thoughts as ideas that are not important in their lives.

This pattern makes us take the content of our mind as literal, which gradually leads us to behave under those thoughts.

Imagine a person who has felt anxiety on the street, for example. This person has come home and has calmed down. The next day she has to go out into the street; the thought "you're going to be nervous, it's going to happen the same as yesterday" crosses her mind, and she begins to take that thought as absolute truth; she concentrates on that thought and begins to observe all the signs that prove him right. Suddenly you notice that you are breathing faster, and your heart rate has increased. He decides to stay home.

This type of behavior can end up creating a pattern of behavior that is quite harmful to the person since they are finally letting themselves be guided by a thought that occurred in a certain circumstance and which they have forgotten; it has brought the sensations they had that day before the present and has isolated thought by giving it the power to decide for it.

The opposite process to cognitive fusion would be that of defusion. Cognitive defusion _ HYPERLINK "https://www.psyciencia.com/video-que-es-la-defusion-cognitiva/" \t "_blank" It allows the person to recognize what a thought, a feeling, or a memory is without taking it as reality, it allows it to be deliteralized.

It is training. You can achieve the goal of observing a thought for what it is, verbal content, in various ways.

One of the different ways you can use if you want to learn to see thoughts for what they are and take something away from them is meditation.

It is not about meditating to become a Buddhist monk, but small exercises can help you in your daily routine.

Meditation exercises can be classified in many ways, but the main one is the one that divides them into formal and informal meditation exercises.

Formal meditation is what we are used to seeing in the movies, and they are exercises in which the only thing you are doing at that moment is meditating. Within this category, there are different approaches; some exercises are not done in the typical lotus flower posture but are done walking or even lying down.

You can dedicate some time every day to formal exercises. If you find it difficult to start, it is best to do it with the guidance of an expert.

On the other hand, informal meditation is carried out while we perform other tasks. You can meditate while taking a shower, walking, or doing the dishes.

The important thing is to get out of your mind for a little while, to become aware that the speech you hear daily inside your head is a continuous flow of linked thoughts that sometimes do not allow you to see reality.

Awareness of your thoughts can be an impulse to carry out many things that now fear you or even to see yourself differently.

Perhaps you have never tried to make that change you are looking for because you have been guided by a thought that told you that you were not capable, that has caused unpleasant sensations and feelings in you and to which you have preferred to pay attention because it seems that the "voice of the experience."

Getting out of our minds, worries, and infinite discourse will allow you to enjoy the present moment more.

Now let's look at some tools that can be useful when applying this theory.

1. Enunciate our thoughts

When we have an intrusive thought that disturbs us, we make a statement as follows; we place the thought at the end of the next sentence, "I am not" or "I am," depending on the thought.

For example, if we think of harming an animal or someone, we should simply accommodate that thought: "I am not an aggressive person, and I do not have to harm anyone."

1. The loss of meaning

This technique consists of continuously repeating a word or phrase that comes to mind when we have negative thoughts in such a way that after repetition, the word being said loses its meaning. Then we must do the same with the thought that bothers us until we make sense of it, and in such a way that it is no longer a thought that we try to run away from but that we will be able to face by constantly repeating it.

These exercises are very useful for separating our reality from those intrusive thoughts that can become annoying. If we make them a habit, the annoying thoughts will likely disappear.

However, how many times have you thought, "what a good time I would be having if I wasn't thinking about this that worries me"? If the answer is "many," then you need a change.

Sometimes the solution is as simple as stopping for a while and allowing yourself to observe yourself, observe your sensations and feelings, discover where they come from, what causes them, and pay attention to what you can control: the now.

correcting your Anxiety Lens

Anxiety is an emotion that everyone experiences in a situation of uncertainty and threat. Prepares the person for scenarios that may have a negative outcome. It is adaptive, and it is good. The problem occurs when it becomes pathological and manifests itself too intensely and frequently. Far from helping to adapt, it blocks the individual, leads to a worse result than desired, and may compromise their physical and mental health.

However, people with an anxiety disorder are essentially phobic about the emotional state of anxiety and go to great lengths to avoid it.

Some people experience a generalized anxiety disorder, excessive anxiety about real-life concerns such as money, relationships, health, career and academic problems, family problems, etc.

Others suffer from social anxiety, continually worrying about the perception of themselves by others, anticipating uncomfortable or embarrassing situations, etc.

Whether you have occasional or generalized anxiety, the good news is that you can take small, effective, and simple daily steps to manage and minimize your anxiety.

Making some basic lifestyle changes can drastically change our state of anxiety.

To treat anxiety, many doctors categorically reject using medications to solve the problem and opt for cognitive behavioral therapy. It is the one that has been studied the most at a scientific level, and that has best demonstrated its effectiveness." To understand what this therapy consists of and give useful advice, it explains in detail the steps necessary to overcome anxiety.

The first step that must be taken or that anyone should do is learn about anxiety since many are unaware that the symptoms they suffer from are caused or caused by anxiety. The first step to recovery is knowing what is happening to them and noticing the symptoms. "Tachycardia, sweat, increased temperature, difficulty sleeping, digestive discomfort, etc., are some of them." Then it would be necessary to discover the causative factors and determine what emotions and anxiety are.

What anxiety does is that the person anticipates very negative consequences just in case they occur. You have to interpret the threat less thoughtfully, be realistic and not magnify it".

Practically:

• Reason if the possibility of the worst happening is so great.

• Ask yourself: "if the worst happened, would it be that bad?".

• Pay attention to problems only when something can be done. "When there is nothing to do, you must continue normal life and attend to other things."

When there is anxiety, attention is continuously focused on the problem, "we don't stop thinking about what worries us.

"The person has to learn to relax, not to focus their attention all the time on the problem. Be alert, but also rest and save resources when nothing can be done".

To achieve this, you have to:

- Force yourself to think about something else.
- Forcing them to do something different to distract themselves.

The interpretation of difficulties as a challenge, rather than a threat". This allows you to face the situation with motivation, leaving aside worry.

Relaxation techniques (progressive muscle, breathing, imagination, among others) also help. The physiological activation is reduced, the muscles are released, etc.

"When these skills are trained, problems start to be solved.

When a person suffers a panic attack, anxiety gets out of control, loses control, and is scared by that lack of control. "Heart rate increases, breathing becomes difficult, hyperventilation, temperature rise, and tremor."

"The autonomic nervous system is triggered and you have to reassure it by transmitting the feeling that there is no danger, that there is no extreme situation and that what is happening is not serious. By changing the focus of attention and the importance we give to panic attack symptoms, they decrease."

The best way to achieve this is:

- Do and think about something else.
- Change the topic of conversation.
- Get to work on something.
- Carry out any activity that allows you to ignore your symptoms.
- Instead of hyperventilating, breathe more slowly.

1. Breathe deeply

Deep diaphragmatic breathing activates our relaxation response, changing our sympathetic nervous system's fight or flight response, the relaxed and balanced response of our parasympathetic nervous system.

Breathe slowly, breathe deeply and regularly. Biofeedback can quickly help you control your breathing. The benefits of improving your breathing are endless, both from a physiological point of view and mentally and emotionally.

2. exercise _

Regular cardiovascular exercise releases endorphins which lead to a reduction in anxiety. A simple walk of 30 or 40 minutes is enough to achieve the beneficial effects and help you control your mood.

You can start today by taking that little walk. Or create a list of physical activities that you like, and do them regularly: running, rowing, rollerblading, walking, cycling, dancing, swimming, surfing, aerobics, kickboxing, and sports like football, tennis, and soccer. Basketball. The options are numerous ...there is no excuse!

3. sleep well

Not getting enough sleep can cause anxiety. If you're having trouble sleeping, try engaging in a relaxing activity before bed tonight, such as taking a warm bath, listening to soothing music, or taking several deep breaths.

And if you're like many people with anxiety whose brains start "buzzing" right before bed, jot down your worries earlier in the day for 10 to 15 minutes, or do a distracting mental exercise to get out of your thoughts, like thinking about things you start with the same letter or similar games.

4. challenge your thought anxious

Fortunately, we can change these thoughts. The first step is to identify them.

Negative thoughts usually come in the form of "what if," "all or nothing" thinking, or "excessive catastrophizing," such as, "What if I don't pass this test?" or "What if the plane crashes?", "What if I make a fool of myself?" It is important to ask yourself:

"Is this concern realistic?" "Is it likely to happen?" "If the worst possible outcome happens, what would be so bad?", "Can I do it?", "What could I do?", "If something bad happens, what could it mean for me? "," "Is this true, or does it just seem that way to me? "What could I do to prepare for what might happen?"

So, reframe or correct what you think would be more accurate, realistic, and adaptable. Conductance Biofeedback can help you control your anxiety and work on eliminating obsessive or recurring thoughts.

5. statements positive

Accurate positive statements can help put things in perspective. Anxiety is a feeling, like any other feeling, and even if you feel bad, you can use some strategies to deal with the states in which that anxiety dominates us.

How? Through our Method, you will find concrete answers and clear and precise guidelines so you can learn to Regain control.

6. Connect with others.

Social support is vital for managing stress and anxiety. Call a loved one, schedule a Skype date, or eat with a close friend. Talking to others can do a lot of good.

7. avoid caffeine

Anxiety management is as much about what you do as it is about what you don't do. And some substances exacerbate anxiety, and caffeine is one of those substances.

8. avoid substances and hallucinogens

While drugs and alcohol can help reduce anxiety in the short term, they often do the opposite in the long term. Even the short-term effect can be detrimental to anxiety, which is not the solution to your problems.

9. do something you enjoy

Participating in enjoyable activities helps calm your anxiety. For example, take that distracting walk, listen to music, or read a book.

10. Rest during your journey

It is also useful to create breaks in your day-to-day. It is enough with a simple change of pace or landscape, enjoying a hobby, stopping to breathe, doing certain "non-mandatory" tasks, etc. A break after exertion can be very refreshing for your mood.

11. solve problems

A quick and easy way to deal with the stressors causing your anxiety is to make a list of these stressors and write down one or two solutions next to each one. It seems basic and absurd, but writing forces you to rationalize things, and you will discover that often not everything is as dark as it seems or as we want to see it.

12. learn to relax

Learn relaxation techniques. There are many ways to achieve the desired emotional and physical deactivation, and we recommend Biofeedback for its objectivity and speed. Still, you can combine this Method and its initial phases based on physiological deactivation with the most effective stress and anxiety control techniques. That's what we offer at Nastia. Again we insist on our goal: Help you regain control.

13. You accept your anxiety

Learn relaxation techniques. There are many ways to achieve the desired emotional and physical deactivation, and we recommend Biofeedback for its objectivity and speed. Still, you can combine this Method and its initial phases based on physiological deactivation with the most effective stress and anxiety control techniques. That's what we offer at Nastia. Again we insist on our goal: Help you regain control.

Acceptance of anxiety does not mean giving up on getting better and living a life of continual anxiety-affected moods. It simply means living with certain unpleasant emotional states that are unavoidable but that we must make transitory.

So if you experience anxiety today, observe it, let it pass, experience it, and deal with it. At least initially, you will prevent a mild anxiety crisis from turning into an acute attack or leading to a panic attack.

By taking small steps – like the ones above – you can minimize anxiety and deal with it effectively. And remember, the solution is within your reach. Increasing your self-control and reducing your anxiety will help you exponentially improve your health and quality of life.

Other techniques to calm anxiety include I don't know Therapy: If you identify a repetitive worrying thought of the type "what if...?", it is best to let it continue, thinking or saying "I don't know.", We will see." You never know what will happen in the future, so there is no need to worry in advance. Example: What if I lose my job? Instead of telling you that it's nonsense or stop thinking, it's better to say, "I don't know, we'll see." The Safe Place: Think of a real or imaginary place that brings you peace, tranquility, and security. Describe it in your imagination with all the details, trying to feel what you would feel with each of your senses if you were there. Stay with it until you feel better. Finally, we have The Four Elements: Earth, rub your feet against the ground and your hands against some surface, feel, feel. Water: create and swallow saliva. Air: Take slow, deep breaths. Fire: the fire of your imagination, you can bring the safe place or any other image that brings you peace.

There are many general tips like the ones we have just seen, but there are other more specific ones. One of the fundamental things to control anxiety is to have a feeling of control and launch a series of cognitive-behavioral strategies. For example, a calendar to time activities, one of the feelings of people who suffer from anxiety is the lack of control, so you have to make them feel that sense of control again and at the same time combine work and leisure or study and leisure depending on what you do. Another "formula" is to write a phrase or word on a piece of paper and place it somewhere visible to help us remember every time we see that word what we want for our lives (peace, well-being, tranquility, joy, optimism, etc.). It is about looking for a signal that helps us focus our attention on lowering the level of anxiety and focusing on the well-being we want for ourselves.

distress tolerance skills

Frustration is the feeling that arises when we don't get what we want; It is about the emotional response that occurs when our projects, expectations, or goals are not met; or our desires and needs are not met.

Frustration is a mixture of anxiety, anguish, helplessness, sadness, or anger that appears when we fail to achieve our goals.

We all experience a normal reaction when things do not go as we expect or wish they would. The problem, as almost always, arises when our reactions to situations that frustrate us generate excessive discomfort; it distances us even more from achieving what we want.

People differ in their ability to tolerate frustration. Some cannot tolerate the slightest delay in the satisfaction of their desires, and they cannot bear any unpleasant feeling or circumstance; that is, they do not tolerate the fact of feeling frustrated. And others, however, have learned to manage it properly, improving their perseverance to achieve their long-term goals.

Frustration is part of life; therefore, learning to relate to and manage it is beneficial.

Work on an emotional level, and train ourselves in the strategies that help us have a greater tolerance for frustration; It will allow us to face the difficulties and limitations that life presents us effectively.

People who learn to tolerate frustration tend to have a lower level of stress; they can remain calm in the face of unforeseen events, not allowing problems to disturb them excessively; In addition, they can accept more easily that pain, suffering, discomfort, or failure are part of life; which means that they act proactively and try to find alternative solutions that allow them to achieve their goals.

In contrast, people whose ability to tolerate frustration is low do not accept things as they are; The unforeseen events that, for the majority, are simply unpleasant inconveniences, they experience as true catastrophes; their perception of the situation is often exaggerated and wrong.

By not supporting the discomfort that things do not turn out as they wish, they tend to become easily demotivated; and in their search for immediate well-being, they tend to abandon their projects prematurely; without taking into account the benefits, they could have in the medium and long term if they managed to manage their feelings differently.

The low tolerance for frustration means that, in the face of any discomfort, we become discouraged and abandon our goals or projects; our desires lose importance.

People with a low tolerance for frustration often confuse their wants with their needs; when they want something, they want it now, without being able to bear the waiting time involved in achieving a goal; It is for this reason that low tolerance for frustration has often been related to difficulty in controlling impulses.

When we cannot tolerate the slightest inconvenience, setback, or delay in satisfying our desires, we risk becoming reactive people who, in the face of adverse circumstances, adopt a passive and negative role, which generates unnecessary Stress and, consequently, greater life dissatisfaction.

However, when we learn to handle frustrations appropriately, our lives are much less stressful and fulfilling; since we can focus all our energy on solving and overcoming the obstacles, we encounter; beyond the exhaust reaction.

Accepting and understanding that frustration is part of our lives is the first step in starting to handle it more appropriately.

All emotions, even those that are not pleasant for us, are part of our life and are natural reactions to negative events that happen to us; ignoring them or trying to eliminate them is not only impossible, but it will also cause us greater emotional suffering.

Acceptance allows us to stop fighting something we cannot change; accepting life as it is presented to us helps us to better deal with difficulties; It is important to remember that accepting is synonymous with resigning, and therefore it does not mean abandoning and stopping trying to achieve what is desired; when you accept, you decide to stop fighting with yourself and with the circumstances to focus on solving the problem.

Learning and developing our tolerance for frustration is a learning process that begins in childhood and never ends; it requires patience and perseverance, but the result is well worth it since tolerating frustration means being able to face the problems and limitations that we have throughout life, despite the annoyances and inconveniences that they cause us; which will allow us to have a more serene and balanced life.

Accept situations and understand that you cannot change what happened, even if you don't like it. That is precisely what radical acceptance is about, a method managed by mental health professionals.

Radical acceptance, classified by experts as a strategy or skill, has the purpose of "accepting the facts of reality without responding with negligent stubbornness" or other similar actions before painful life events.

Radical acceptance is not approving something, and rather it is to fully accepting with your mind and body that you cannot change the facts in the present. By accepting something radically (things out of our control), we prevent getting stuck in unhappiness, bitterness, and sadness, and we can stop suffering.

Through this emotional ability, many people can manage to face extremely painful circumstances. It is a powerful skill that helps to live with painful things, and it's like lubricating our ability to handle situations to prevent emotional pain from turning into suffering.

To avoid further distress.

Please recognize that the uncomfortable came into my life because it is part of life. In life, we will have to live pleasant and unpleasant moments. Things we want, expect, and things that surprise us and do not expect. From the perspective of radical acceptance, when I accept that this happened to me, I will be able to have better strategies to cope with it. Accepting is not surrendering to pain, and it is not staying without doing anything but not hiding reality.

The distress tolerance skill can be applied to different situations in life. For example, in a breakup mourning, in which the denial stage occurs and the beliefs that "this can't be happening to me," "I didn't prepare for this," or "I don't deserve it." "

From radical acceptance, I focus on my time of pain and what my emotions are telling me. I focus on my present above all. In living in the here and now

Another strategy of radical acceptance is the connection with the senses since, in this way, the person can make a link between their mind and body and thus understand what hurts, where, and why.

Since the disconnection I suffered, I have become attached to suffering. So, radical acceptance is an invitation not to get attached to suffering.

On the other hand, in the case of mourning for death, radical acceptance proposes to feel the pain and allows it to be there as long as necessary.

"Radical acceptance is not that you will be perfectly fine, and it is the opposite. It's making peace with the pain. The pain will be less and less because I manage it."

First, it is important to remember that reality is uncomfortable and cannot be changed.

Similarly, practice acceptance with the mind, body, and spirit. This is through techniques such as mindfulness, relaxation, and others.

Also, open steps to the sensations that appear in the face of disappointment, sadness, or mourning. To later recognize that life has value, even when there is pain.

Finally, when you feel some resistance to practicing acceptance, make a "pros and cons" list.

The help of mental health professionals with knowledge of this method is very important.

"Help in therapy is essential. Many other things can be alternated and are very good, but therapy is not replaced by anything.

In addition, he invited people to acknowledge their concerns and take the action of going to psychotherapy.

It is recommended to do so by presenting the following signs that you identify within these signs that our body and ourselves:

· Faced with persistent feelings of helplessness and sadness.

· Excessive worries and pessimistic thoughts.

· Excessive consumption of alcohol and illicit drugs also has repercussions on others.

· Difficulty concentrating on daily tasks and activities.

The current stigma in mental health issues causes people not to seek professional help when necessary, which is why these problems always continue.

ANXIETY RELAPSE AND PREVENTION

A relapse means the reappearance of the signs and symptoms of a disease after a period of improvement. Relapses are very common in major depressive disorders and anxiety problems. Could you take it as a learning process when it's wrong again? Many times without realizing it, you have neglected yourself and have stopped doing the strategies you put in place to improve. If you have overcome depression or an anxiety problem, take care of yourself very seriously, think of it as a philosophy of life, and take time to do small self-care routines. Anxiety is so present in our day-to-day life that it sometimes doesn't take much extra to overwhelm us. At that time, we look for ways to solve the problem. We go to the doctor or psychologist and put strategies in place... But afterward, how can we prevent relapses?

If you continue doing the same after a relapse, do not expect your situation to change over time; try to be an active agent in your improvement process. We can get hold of and train a series of tools to help us with the mission so that anxiety does not return, and this article will discuss them and how you can use them to avoid a relapse.

Observe the warning signs and symptoms that make you realize you are in a relapse. The most frequent are the inability to feel pleasure, anhedonia, apathy, tiredness, sleeping badly or sleeping a lot, negative thoughts about the future, etc.

To prevent this type of problem, it is important to include in our daily life other types of activities that help us eliminate this type of negative thoughts and help release loads of anxiety and Stress. Within these, you can find

Do exercise. It does not have to be in the gym regularly, and going for a walk or practicing sports such as Yoga or Pilates would be enough. By exercising, we secrete endorphins, and thus we manage to increase our mood.

Letting off steam on time helps manage our emotions with friends, professionals, or trusted people. But not everything revolves around that relapse. Talk about other things, and ask other people to tell you neutral or positive things.

Keep a journal of how we feel. Write down all the positive things that happen to you.

Think positively. That is, realizing if we have irrational thoughts that do not help us get what we want. An example is the unscientific thoughts of the all, nothing, need, can't type. And changing these words to most of the time, I can, I'm going to try will help you not feel so bad and see things much more objectively.

Do rewarding activities even if we don't feel like it. The desire usually appears later. Valuable activities, that is, activities that benefit us or those around us, housework, favors, an assignment for someone. And planned activities that have a specific schedule and make us leave the house and aim to reduce negative thought loops.

Be related. It is common that after a moment is shared with someone who fills you with energy, that person who, after spending time with her, brings you positive things, raises your mood, thinks in a way that helps you and you see things not so black.

Get up and go to bed at the same time. Try to regulate your routines before going to bed, do something relaxing that tells your body that it is time to rest.

Dedicate some time each day to rest, observe ourselves, and be aware of how we are, how we feel, and what we can do to take better and better care of ourselves.

Focus on the present. Don't beat yourself up over past mistakes, and don't start predicting the future.

Take care of the messages you send yourself. After a small mistake, don't talk bad to yourself and don't say offensive things to yourself. Change the way you criticize yourself for a more positive message.

Learn to be assertive. Start expressing what you want while respecting the rights of others and your own.

What can you do to be more relaxed?

Normalize thoughts, eliminate things like I have to, and I should, etc. Beware of catastrophic thoughts. Every time you anticipate, it can help you think this is not happening to me yet. If it happens, I will face it, and I have many more resources than I think.

Practice relaxation daily. Learn to breathe abdominally, a very useful tool you can use anytime.

Relax every day with activities that make you disconnect.

Try to slow down all-day routines: walk slowly, eat quietly, and focus your attention on the task at hand.

Reduce the consumption of caffeine, tea, chocolate, and sweets. Take care of your diet without obsessing.

Face the situations that make you anxious. Using the breath and self-instruction (what you say to yourself). Write a series of thoughts you will repeat to yourself every time you face your fears, such as I can, I am capable, I have done very well other times, etc.

And if you see that trying to make changes on your own does not improve, go to the doctor, psychiatrist, and psychologist for guidance and help in your recovery process. Be clear that relapses come out.

Also, the first thing to remember is that our effectiveness in preventing relapses will depend on the treatment we have followed to manage anxiety at first. This may not seem relevant, but it is the most important thing. Yes, if we have chosen to take some psychoactive drug, it will be more difficult to prevent relapses ourselves. I explain. With pharmacological therapy, we ingest a pill that lowers our anxiety levels. Still, if it is not combined with psychological intervention, we will not have other anxiety management strategies other than taking medication. However, if we have gone to a quality psychologist, they have probably provided us with various emotional control resources to implement in situations where our balance is compromised. This way, we can apply them, far from resorting to medicine. That is why, although it requires more effort, psychological intervention is more recommended to avoid relapses. If we have chosen a suitable psychologist from a cognitive-behavioral current, we will have acquired tools to manage our thoughts and emotions throughout the therapy. But, like all the skills we learn throughout our lives, we will have to continue practicing them if we do not want to lose them. Thus, continuing with some exercises, even if more spaced and frequent, will be the first step to preventing relapses. Think, for example, of how, when we learn a language, if we stop speaking it, we quickly lose fluency, right? In this case, the same thing happens: if we stop applying emotional control strategies, it will cost us more to use them when we need them.

That is, we must try to maintain the changes obtained in therapy. The work does not end when the intervention ends, and the psychologist discharges us, and it continues daily, so our emotional health depends largely on ourselves.

Not only do we have to continue practicing, but we also have to remember the information we have received in therapy with psychoeducation. For this reason, let us not banish the role of thoughts in the emotional process to the drawer of oblivion. You already know that we all have maladaptive thoughts, so you must be attentive to identify them, classify them, and question them to the extent that they seem suspicious.

Do not forget that not every day, the sun shines with the same strength. I explain. Every one of us has bad days, and somehow this condition is intrinsic to our nature. Where we have a choice is how to deal with them or not anticipate that a day that starts crooked will continue to be crooked. Many days that start crooked continue to be crooked by our anxiety, which makes us lose our heads and plays the role of sorceress so that the phenomenon of the self-fulfilling prophecy occurs.

Finally, nothing happens if you need to go to the psychologist again. In no way is it a failure, nor does it mean that you have lost everything you have advanced up to that moment... It is preferable to do it before the anxiety becomes stronger!

STRESS AND MORE PROBLEMS

We have all heard of Stress, and many have even mentioned that we are "stressed," but ultimately, what is Stress?

Stress can be defined as a set of physiological reactions that occur when a person suffers a state of nervous tension, a product of various situations in the workplace or personal: overwork, anxiety, traumatic situations that have been experienced, etc. Stress is a state of physical and emotional tension caused as a reaction to a stimulus or pressure, whether positive or negative. It is a state of defense that, in small doses, helps the body react and adapt to events.

A normal stress level is considered healthy and even positive since it helps stimulate people to act on the stimuli of daily life. However, when stress is excessive or not adequately controlled, it can cause mental exhaustion problems, such as irritability and anxiety or psychosomatic disorders.

A psychosomatic disorder is a physiological illness caused by emotional causes, usually Stress. Some of the most frequent psychosomatic disorders caused by stress are headaches, insomnia, muscular tension, digestive and cardiac problems, dizziness...

- Normal Stress: the physiological reactions that occur in our body in certain situations and are defined as Stress are normal to a certain extent. A little stress and anxiety can help us face and overcome some difficult situations.

•

- Pathological Stress: when Stress occurs intensely for prolonged periods, it is very likely to cause physical and psychological problems, transforming into chronic and harmful Stress that can cause crying spells, depression, and various physical conditions.

- Post-traumatic Stress: is the one that occurs after a person has experienced some terrifying event, such as a traffic accident or a natural disaster. As a result of these traumas, the person often has terrifying thoughts related to the situation they experienced. This type of Stress can appear in people of all ages, but children are particularly prone to it.

•

- Job stress: job stress is a set of harmful emotional and physical reactions that occur when the demands in the workplace exceed the workers' resources, capabilities, or needs. According to a study by the WHO, 28% of European workers suffer from work stress, and 20% suffer from the syndrome called "burnout."

There are many causes of Stress, although not all have to be negative. Normally, it appears when a person is faced with one or more situations that exceed their resources and are unable to overcome them, causing some emotional and physical symptoms.

There is also positive stress, which occurs when it helps the person to adapt to the environment.

When we perceive a threat or danger, real or not, our body prepares for two quick and effective solutions: fight or flight. The autonomic nervous system is involved in them, responsible for the organic functions of our body that occur involuntarily, such as beating the heart or breathing. This is divided into two: the sympathetic nervous system, which prepares us for action, and the parasympathetic, which regulates the activities of our body at rest.

Faced with the threatening stimulus, the sympathetic system produces a hormonal response, generating greater adrenaline and cortisol. The first increases heart rate, dilates the pupils and bronchial tubes and makes us sweat. The second hormone increases the sugar level in the blood and suppresses the activity of the immune system.

This happens temporarily since the parasympathetic nervous system is responsible for putting "everything in order." Still, it is easy to imagine that when this whole process is repeated too often or continuously, it can have harmful consequences for our health.

Distinguishing between an acceptable dose of Stress and an excessive one is not always easy. We are used to running around, multitasking, and often facing challenges, so it is important to pay attention not only to our moods but also to some physical symptoms, such as the following that They warn us that daily stresses are affecting us:

· Frequent headaches.

· Diarrhea or constipation.

· Fatigue excessive, decay.

· Jaw stiff, muscles tense.

· http://www.sanitas.es/sanitas/seguros/es/particulares/biblioteca-de-salud/Lesiones/prevencion-recuperacion/insomnio-riesgo-lesion.htmlInsomnia http://www.sanitas.es/sanitas/seguros/es/particulares/biblioteca-de-salud/Lesiones/prevencion-recuperacion/insomnio-riesgo-lesion.htmlor sleepiness

· Unusual weight variations

Our brain also sends us other alarm signals such as demotivation, lack of sexual desire, irritability, anxiety or forgetfulness, and memory delays.

Among the risks of chronic Stress are lowered defenses, high blood pressure, diabetes, heart failure, acne, eczema, depression, anxiety, or problems derived from constant tension such as muscle contractures or bruxism clenching the jaw too often and unconsciously when we sleep. Being constantly stressed can also make us gain weight since it affects the regulation of our impulses and emotions, causing us to opt for delicious foods with little nutritional value. This lack of control often leads to other harmful habits and behaviors, such as smoking or drinking alcohol in excess to try to relax, with its corresponding negative consequences.

Some studies state that work stress, one of the most frequent, increases the risk of developing coronary heart disease by 68% and that of suffering a myocardial infarction by 23%. In the long term, stress can lead to serious health problems, making us feel more stressed. Prevention and treatment are very important through psychological therapy and support such as meditation, physical activity, and good nutrition.

Trusting our ability to deal with situations that affect us is a good starting point to begin controlling Stress. The next thing is to ask ourselves what we can do to reduce it: consult a specialist, practice mindfulness, do moderate exercise, look for another job, do some pleasant activity at the end of the day such as walking or reading... The alternatives are many, and it is worth putting them into practice when necessary. A life with less Stress is a healthier life in every way.

In general, the consequences of Stress affect, first of all, the person who suffers from it. But, it is also normal to affect people in the immediate environment: family, friends, co-workers... Initially, it is an emotional repercussion; if a person suffers, family and friends who are part of their emotional circle will also suffer. The repercussions of Stress can extend beyond the particular area where the stressful situation originates; that is, a stressful work situation will, first of all, affect the person and their entire work environment, but the family and social environment of the individual may also be affected since he will transmit his state of mind and his problems to family and closest friends. The same can occur in conflictive situations in the family, which will inevitably have repercussions in the work environment.

In the personal sphere, the consequences of Stress can be defined as those that affect the individual and can suppose integral damage to his person. Manifestations can be:

· Disorders somatic

· Disorders psychics

· Increased consumption of psychotropic medications (hypnotics, sedatives, anxiolytics, antidepressants) and others (analgesics, etc.)

· consequences of certain behaviors :

o Food: obesity, with the corresponding metabolic, cardiac, and joint repercussions, sleep apnea... Anorexia with weight loss (with possible anemia)

o Alcohol intake: organic and psychic repercussionTobacco: pulmonary and cardiovascular repercussion

· Increased risk of accidents (at work, traffic, domestic) due to reduced attention or reckless behavior with disregard for danger (for example, risky driving, ignoring protection measures at work or traffic signs...)

· Others:-

Entering into conflict with oneself by questioning ideas, thoughts, and life trajectories, being able to experience negative feelings towards oneself (self-blame) with increased anxiety.

Make past, "unresolved" conflict situations present again, which increases its effects in the context of a stressful situation.-

Feeling of unhappiness, bitterness, and loss of meaning in life. - Abandonment of oneself in all senses. Possibility of delaying medical consultations due to illness, healthy habits...- Loss of hobbies. Isolation

The family environment cause problems in the couple's relationship: affective and sexual deterioration. Risk of rupture especially concerning alcohol, gambling, or other addictions. Problems with children:

- Deterioration of their relationship
- Negative effect on their education
- Studies and control of their social relations

Economic deterioration of the family environment. Deterioration or loss of relationships with other relatives (parents, siblings...) The global repercussion on the family unit.

As for the repercussions in the workplace, there are

Alterations in the working day's schedule, such as arriving late or general situations to be absent from work before the normal departure time. Absenteeism Sick leave from work, prolonged beyond what is strictly necessary, often concerning illness behavior Repercussions on colleagues due to absenteeism, due to having to take over the tasks of the absent colleague. Deterioration of relationships with bosses and colleagues due to:

Less patience in dealing with colleagues and bosses. More frequent discussions with them. Bad manners in relationships. Putting more pressure than usual on subordinates in carrying out tasks. Frequent irritability and complaints towards bosses, colleagues, the work organization system, etc. Demand greater attention from colleagues towards oneself by continually making them participants in our state of mind or conflictive situation. Decreased performance at work with the delay of usual tasks. Indifference to the results of the work. Greater risk of occupational accidents

And in the social sphere, there is less interest in participating in social activities, deterioration or rupture of relationships with friends, neighbors... Decrease or loss of commitment to the norms of society and increased risk of accidents

Entering more specifically in terms of its clinical effects, it is known that Stress maintained over time can accelerate the progression of chronic diseases and trigger numerous physical illnesses and mental disorders:

1. Alterations and pathologies physical :

·   Immune system: hyperactivation reduces the immune competence of the body, which increases the risk of suffering from infections (flu, herpes...) or allergies. It can also lead to a worse evolution of immunological diseases such as cancer.

·   Digestive and gastrointestinal disorders: the digestive system stops working regularly, so many of its functions are slowed down or paralyzed. Stomach pain, diarrhea, gas, constipation, heartburn, heavy digestion, vomiting... In the long run, there is a greater probability of developing diseases such as ulcerative colitis, irritable bowel, or gastric ulcer.

·   Cardiovascular system: Stress is a direct risk factor for coronary heart disease, as it increases heart rate and blood pressure and accelerates the narrowing of the arteries due to the accumulation of substances such as cholesterol in the blood. It also encourages harmful habits such as increased consumption of alcohol or tobacco and less practice of physical exercise, in addition to unhealthy eating.

·   Endocrine system: Stress raises the sugar concentration in the blood, which increases the probability of being overweight and obese, risk factors for diabetes.

·   Respiratory system: the prolonged increase in the rate of breathing can lead to episodes of hyperventilation and a feeling of shortness of breath.

·   Reproductive system and sexuality: such as menstrual irregularities, increased probability of a miscarriage, decreased fertility, reduced or absent sexual desire, erectile dysfunction, etc.

·   Dermatological problems: the body does not correctly regulate the hydration of the epidermis, and dryness favors the appearance of dermatitis or hair loss. Other common skin problems include eczema or acne and an increased risk of psoriasis flare-ups in those with psoriasis.

2. Alterations in psychological and mental _

- Anxiety disorders: Anxiety and Stress are not synonymous, but Stress can trigger an anxiety reaction, which is an unpleasant emotion that arises in the face of that threat due to the possibility that it implies a negative outcome. Anxiety is not completely negative and fulfills a function as an emotional reaction that puts the body on alert and encourages it to activate its defense mechanisms in the face of a conflict. It becomes a health problem if excessive or disproportionate, altering the person's psychophysiological state, well-being, behavior, and daily life. In these cases, you can get to suffer these disorders:

- Generalized anxiety: very intense anxiety symptoms occur without a real cause that provokes them and without control by the affected person.

- Panic attack: intense fear suddenly appears accompanied by a feeling of loss of control due to a sudden increase in symptoms such as chest pain, fear of dying, dizziness, tremor, feeling of shortness of breath...

- Phobia: the intense and distressing panic that is felt in the face of some circumstances or stimuli.

- Obsessive-compulsive disorder: intrusive or obsessive ideas or thoughts that the person cannot control. They cause strong anguish that is tried to neutralize with repetitive behaviors, which become rituals.

· Stress occurs when a traumatic situation in which the person has suffered or may have suffered extreme physical or psychological damage alters their personal and work life.

- Mood disorders: episodes of prolonged Stress often trigger disorders such as depression, characterized by persistent feelings of sadness, anxiety, emptiness, hopelessness, pessimism, guilt, irritability, and restlessness. In addition, depression reduces stress resistance, so both enhance each other. Other mental disorders associated with high levels of anxiety and Stress are eating disorders -anorexia, bulimia-bipolar disorder, hypochondria, or pernicious behaviors -consumption or addiction to alcohol, tobacco, or anxiolytics-.

- Psychophysiological disorders: negative emotions are somatized, and the physical alterations seen above are suffered without a clear or defined cause: muscular problems, tiredness, headaches, hypertension, eczema...

SELF-DISCIPLINE WHY IS SO IMPORTANT.

One of the main characteristics of self-discipline is the ability to forego instant and immediate gratification in favor of greater profit or more satisfying results, even if this requires time and effort.

Self-discipline gives us the power to stick to our decisions and follow through on them without wavering and is, therefore, one of the important prerequisites for achieving goals. Self-discipline is the ability to move forward, stay motivated, and take action regardless of how you feel, physically or emotionally. You're showing it when you intentionally choose to seek something better for yourself, and you do so despite factors like distractions, hard work, or unfavorable odds. Self-discipline is different from self-motivation or willpower. Motivation and willpower contribute to this, as do persistence, the ability to follow through on your intentions, and hard work.

Possessing self-discipline allows us to choose and then persevere with actions, thoughts, and behaviors that lead to improvement and success.

It also gives us the power and inner strength to overcome addictions and laziness and follow up on everything.

Contrary to common belief, self-discipline is not serious and limited behavior or a restrictive lifestyle. It is a very important ingredient for success in our lives. It is expressed as perseverance, the ability not to give up despite failure and setbacks, self-control, and resistance to temptations and distractions that tend to get in the way of achieving goals. It is one of the most important pillars of real and stable success.

This ability leads to self-confidence, self-esteem, inner strength, happiness, and satisfaction. On the other hand, a lack of self-discipline can lead to failure, loss, health and relationship problems, obesity, and more.

Self-discipline is useful in many areas of our lives.

For example, it pushes you to do high-quality work, even when you don't feel like it. It helps you meet and achieve the difficult goals you set for yourself. Self-discipline also allows you to keep moving toward great success, despite what others may see as seemingly insurmountable odds.

Self-discipline is like a muscle: the more you work on developing and using it, the stronger it will become.

However, it is equally important not to start with overly ambitious goals. Instead, set small goals and slowly increase the challenge level over time. The more you practice, the better you will become.

Follow these five steps to start developing your self-discipline:

1. Choose a goal

Start by choosing a single goal you want to focus on to build self-discipline.

For example, maybe you want to start exercising every night or read a leadership book weekly to improve your skills. You could even practice self-discipline on small goals, like concentrating on a job for an hour without checking your messages or avoiding unhealthy foods for a day.

Remember, starting small is the best way to start building your self-discipline. As your discipline strengthens, you can extend the focus to more areas of your life.

2. Find your motivation

Once you have chosen a goal, list why you want to achieve it, and try to express these reasons positively.

So instead of saying, "I want to exercise three times a week to lose weight," say, "I want to exercise, so I have the energy to play with my kids and work successfully." Or, instead of saying, "I want to take this task off my to-do list," say, "I want to do this so I can meet my goals, receive praise from my boss, and feel satisfied with my day's work."

When you list why you want to accomplish something, it will be much easier for you to get the job done.

3. Identify obstacles

Now you need to identify the obstacles you are likely to face when working towards your goal and devise a strategy to overcome each one.

For example, imagine your goal is to read a weekly leadership book to improve your skills. In the past, you have faced several obstacles in reaching this goal. For example, it's hard to find time each night to read when you find a book you like. Your time is occupied late into the night between work, dinner, and the kids. And you get distracted by the messages that arrive while you read.

Once you've identified the obstacles, come up with a strategy to overcome each one. In this example, you could do the following:

Instead of going to a bookstore, spend an hour looking at leadership books online. Find several that interest you and have good reviews. Order them all at once and download them to an eBook reader or tablet, so you always have a book on hand to read.

Find more time in your day to focus on reading. Perhaps you could read during lunch or while you wait to pick up your children from school. Turn off your phone when you want to focus on reading.

Often our self-discipline falls apart because we haven't identified the obstacles we'll face in achieving our goals and haven't developed strategies to overcome them. When these obstacles appear, we are not prepared to deal with them, which shakes our resolve. Don't skip this step!

4. Replace old habits

When developing self-discipline, we often try to break a bad habit and replace it with something more productive. However, breaking that habit can leave a hole and be tied to a certain time of day or routine. If we don't replace that habit with something else, its absence becomes even more conspicuous.

A good example is if you are trying to stop shopping online when you take a break at work. This bad habit destroys your focus and attention because you will likely be online for 20-30 minutes.

Once you've decided to stop, identify a new behavior you can engage in when you need a quick break. Instead of shopping online, you can do some stretching in your office, grab a cup of coffee, or take a quick walk outside. These behaviors will help support your goal and strengthen your self-discipline instead of leaving you with nothing to do on your break.

5. Monitor your progress

As you work on her self-discipline, pay attention to how you feel as she develops and strengthens. You may feel free, happy, proud, and full of energy.

Also, consider keeping a journal to write down your self-discipline goals and track your progress. This reinforces the positive changes you're making in your life and gives you a record you can look back on to see the progress you've made.

Over time, your self-discipline will strengthen, and you can apply it to many other areas of your life.

Try to avoid distractions when you start working on your self-discipline. Make it more difficult to participate in the activity you try to avoid. For example, if you need the self-discipline to focus at work instead of looking at social media, use internet blockers, so these sites are unavailable during work hours.

It is important to reward yourself when you experience success.

Celebrating your accomplishments will keep things fun and strengthen your determination to keep going.

Don't let the fear of failure or an occasional setback get you down. We all experience setbacks and failures; it's part of life! Admit that you made a mistake, learn the lesson, take it seriously and move on.

Do Not Wait to Feel Like It; dump All Your Excuses

The person with a doctorate in the art of excuses resorts to them as a defense mechanism. Making use of the most outlandish pretext and justification for each mistake or incompetence is a way of hiding insecurities, of protecting one's ego.

Excuses corner the brain in the basement of fear. Thus, whoever resorts to them for almost every circumstance limits their growth, responsibility with their lives, and human potential because the habit of excuses is like a virus that sickens the person putting chains to change, to the obligation to take care of oneself maturely.

"I couldn't finish the report because my computer was infected with a Trojan," "I didn't go to the job interview because the train had a breakdown and I couldn't get there, "I know I told you we would go on that trip, but now I have to help my parents»... Behind these and other equally false pretexts lies something more than dishonesty. It is the fear of facing certain realities that one should deal with for their well-being, dignity, and happiness.

Making excuses is the easiest way to face any compromising situation. If we have forgotten an important appointment, it is always better to blame providence, that car breakdown, that sudden illness that has us in bed.

Let us see, however, what dimensions specifically trace this behavior:

- Better to postpone than face (procrastination as a defense mechanism). If something demands a lot from us, if it is going to put us to the test, it is better to leave it for tomorrow. Before dealing with what makes us feel insecure, the wisest thing for these people is to postpone it as long as possible (and credible).

- Safety and comfort before anything else (the fear factor). The person used to making excuses not only lives but hibernates in his comfort zone. Everything beyond is secondary, as well as threatening.

- We want instant gratification. Lounging on the couch is more comfortable than going out for a workout. Checking email or Facebook is easier now than doing that project you've been putting off. Eating chocolate cake is tastier at this point than eating a vegetable salad.

- afraid of something. Fear of not doing it correctly, failure, fear of the unknown, and, most importantly, fear of not being able to finish successfully. That makes us want to put it off, doing something simple and safe instead.

- Postponing something is easy: There are no immediate negative consequences. We will surely pay for it later, but for now, nothing bad will happen. It's easy to skip that activity, stay in that comfort zone, and save yourself the pain of not getting it done.

- Overestimate our future productivity. We have a long list of things we plan to do, and we think it's okay to procrastinate because we'll do it later and even better than now. We believe that we will be incredibly productive and much more focused at another time than right now. But when that future arrives, we are still unable to finish, or worse still, unable to start.

- The reward is still unattainable. Achieving the body you want will not be achieved with an exercise session. It is the constancy that generates the reward. But at this time, it is still far from your immediate reach. In contrast, postponing action brings an immediate reward.

As we have already been able to glimpse, the roots of the bad art of making excuses often sink into the heart of fear or the insecurity of those who resort to the pretext to safeguard their ego or comfortable position in their comfort zone. Sometimes, of course, an excuse is nothing more than a lie, a vile strategy with which to hide certain realities.

Be that as it may, and even if we are the ones who sometimes resort to excuses for not making the changes we should, it is appropriate to take into account certain keys. Reflecting on the following points may be helpful in this type of situation.

The main problem is that when we repeatedly use an excuse, we become convinced that we are incapable of undertaking a certain task; we believe that we cannot. With excuses, we set ourselves non-existent limits, which we have created. We limit our ability to overcome difficulties and challenges,... our ability to grow as human beings. And, in the end, we end with that hackneyed phrase: It's just that I am like that! a self-destructive affirmation that becomes a firm belief with no possibility of modification. Are you going to limit your progress in life, you are going to resign yourself to not achieving your goals and objectives, and you are going to put aside your dreams as an excuse?

I propose that you stop justifying yourself, that you abandon your excuses, that you determine to go beyond what you think limits you. And why don't you start by analyzing how you have overcome the excuses you have given during the day? For example, look at the reasons you've given yourself to go to the gym, get that work done, take your mom to the doctor, visit that sick neighbor, eat a little healthier, walk to work, and help your child with homework... You may think that they are little things that go nowhere. But if we get used to lying to ourselves with excuses for these small daily tasks, our minds will act the same when faced with great responsibilities or more ambitious challenges. Because, as I said before, the problem is that we create our excuses.

To change our tendency to excuse ourselves when something doesn't feel like it, scares us, or requires too much effort, I invite you to go little by little. Perhaps starting with these little things that we leave for another day every day because 'today my back hurts and I can't go to the gym, tomorrow I'll start the diet that today I can't go shopping, on the weekend I'll see my mother and tell me about the doctor, I'm very busy today, ….' I encourage you to replace the excuse with: Yes, I will do it! To not let your mind work to think what excuse I can or 'I can use for not doing it. Be faster than your excuses, take control of your decisions, and find powerful reasons to do it! I invite you to say yes, I can!

This way, we will begin by educating our thoughts with these small acts when we are presented with a great challenge. Instead of looking for an excuse, we will look for a way to tackle it. We will ask ourselves, what can I do to achieve that goal? In short, instead of looking for the excuse, we will look for the how.

And to achieve success in this exercise, we must be patient and constant. Because we cannot expect to achieve something overnight, we have to go little by little. Small changes encourage us to continually show our minds that we can do it because we have looked for the way, the way instead of the excuse.

For this reason, we provide you with some tips to avoid excuses and increasingly stop shielding ourselves with them.

· Every time we detect someone giving us an excuse, it is important not to let it go. The best thing to do is to confront, to force whoever is in front of us to be honest, especially with themselves.

· You have to show that an excuse is a lie respectfully, but a lie that the person tells himself —> I didn't go to that interview because I missed the subway—>I didn't go to that interview because I wouldn't know how to handle a new rejection.

· If excuses are your lifeline, jump in and learn to swim. Many people resort to the most imaginative justifications for not facing what scares them and what they postpone. If someone wants to be respected and, above all, feel good about themselves, they must put excuses aside and simply act, face, resolve, transform...

Do Not Wait For the Right Feeling or Time

It happens to all of us that we have fears: fear of not being sufficiently prepared, fear of failure, fear of not knowing how to manage certain situations... And we choose to stay where we are, eternally preparing ourselves to achieve that dream goal. I have spoken to you on occasions about that comfort zone that welcomes us and makes us feel comfortable, that comfort zone that stops us from going a little further. On this occasion, I am not talking about this area but about that completely different situation, in which we are not comfortable, from which we want to get out, but we do not dare! We think it is better to wait for a better economic, family, or work moment... And so, we let the days, weeks, months, years go by... until when? What are we waiting for? I assure you that no one will take the step for us. It is our task... And, many times, it is we who, with our steps and decision, will make that moment a good one, that this is the right time.

Many of us have found that there is never the right time, and we never know when the last time will be. Leaving pride behind and knowing how to set aside differences are important aspects of living fully and taking advantage of our loved ones or any moment in our lives that terrifies us. We fear making a decision respectfully.

What often happens is that things happen, that time aligns with the desire, and suddenly they arise. But they are very unexpected things, even sometimes not planned. These surprise us, make us happy, and may be maintained over time.

There are plans to which we add aspects or enrich them as we go:

We improvise and find the way.

But there are also plans or goals that perhaps we have had in mind for years and have not done because they mean so much to us that we want to find the right time.

Tomorrow may be too late to apologize, too late to try, too late to believe, too late for a hug, too late for an "I love you," too late for an "I miss you" that will last forever. ...

And this is terrible, more than anything, because we do not give importance to life when our hearts are fresh. But tomorrow, someone around you may send a last message or say a few last words without knowing it. And it can be you too.

Then you will ask yourself what his last message, his last words, or his last hug was, and you want it to be something that moves, demonstrates, and sincerely expresses all the love that unites us in this world.

Be that as it may, I hope you have already fixed the roof before it rains so that the moment of saying goodbye does not catch you off guard.

Because "it's never too late" always comes too soon. And when that happens, it hurts. But, although it always hurts, having enjoyed being with the people we love helps us not to add regret to the pain.

Not being able to say goodbye is scary, very scary. But it is that since our life had a beginning, we know that it will have an end and, however, we stop getting excited, doing what we are passionate about, and hugging those we love too easily.

Be that as it may, I hope you have already fixed the roof before it rains so that the moment of saying goodbye does not catch you off guard.

Because "it's never too late" always comes too soon. And when that happens, it hurts. But, although it always hurts, having enjoyed being with the people we love helps us not to add regret to the pain.

Not being able to say goodbye is scary, very scary. But it is that since our life had a beginning, we know that it will have an end and, however, we stop getting excited, doing what we are passionate about, and hugging those we love too easily.

Ease that scares us and a fear that does not help at all, more than anything because it makes us feel the need to close our eyes and "convince ourselves" that we still have time, that our hearts are fresh, and that nothing bad has to happen...

But the reality is that it happens, that we all have to say goodbye in one way or another, and, when this happens, saying goodbye is more painful than if before it we have wasted time, we have drowned words, and we have forgotten kisses, good morning and the hugs.

If we postpone something just because it doesn't excite us much, that doesn't matter... It is vital if we want to do something because it moves us a lot and we are afraid of not having the perfect conditions, it is the most appropriate time to start!

Just as last week, we said that it is better to do more and think less, leading us to create a permanent habit where we simply launch ourselves to conquer what we want.

So, if it's for money, today you can start saving even if you can't make much. If it's because you want to wait for the right partner, check if you can start on your own if it's because you don't have the time, what things could you stop doing? What is not a priority?

Even if it is an hour a day that you can dedicate to the idea, that will add up, and over time it will become a snowball that gains strength if it motivates you a lot.

We will never be ready emotionally, intellectually, socially, or personally.

So if we are waiting for perfection in ourselves to start something, maybe we are losing valuable time start something.

If we are preparing ourselves and consciously know that we have postponed something because we want to be better and are going towards that, then it is perfect! The focus here is to observe ourselves and see if we postpone something out of fear because we don't believe we are sufficiently prepared or because of exaggerated perfectionism.

Sometimes planning a lot is incredibly useful, but sometimes without so much mind and so many complications, great things can be achieved! If you have been preparing for this new situation for a long time, jump!

If you think you still have time to acquire more preparation: start with slow steps but firm... towards your goal without deviating from the goal!

But never stand still, waiting... And always! Take advantage of the lessons that life offers you every day... Don't forget that bird that had to flee forced by the storm and that found its particular paradise.

When circumstances are the ones that force you to take that step, do it without fear, and step firmly... who tells you not to find your dream paradise thanks to that change?

After all, you have a well-thought-out plan, and as soon as the opportunity presents itself, you will start to carry it out. In the meantime, you have to prepare for this. You can't just start. You will not try to take pictures until you buy a piece of good equipment (after all, it will make you a professional photographer); you won't start running because you can't afford special designer shoes; you will not go to work (although you should), because economic conditions are below your expectations; You will not go on a date, because that man does not adhere to your ideal...

In fantasizing with imaginary visions, we are experts, and a little worse, we are given to try to take a small step to carry them out.

In the same way, the acceptance of the fact that what we have is enough to change our lives. Because, if you have to work, it has to be in a renowned company; if you have to run a business, it has to be very profitable from the beginning; if you have to paint, they have to be works of art.

Few remember that the greatest in this world began with something unattractive. The passion? It comes after. First is work. Waiting for manna to fall from heaven will not stop us from being hungry.

Exercises for Developing and Boosting Self-Discipline

Self-discipline is necessary to maintain a good level and quality of life, as it keeps you from self-destructive behaviors and focused on your goals.

That is why we want to help you improve your self-discipline through habits you need to develop and make part of your daily life.

Implementing habits completely requires your will and desire to improve for your benefit. However, sometimes you can always ask for help from someone close to you or even a health professional such as a psychologist who can help us.

When you work towards big goals without exercising your will, you risk failing, weakening your self-discipline.

That is why you must create the habit of setting goals and objectives for yourself in the short, medium, and long term. That every day you can experience satisfaction as a result of achieving such goals and objectives.

This will spark motivation, and you will continue to strengthen your self-discipline.

Secondly, you must maintain a balance both physically and mentally. Remember that a healthy body allows for a healthy mind.

If you don't take care of your physical health, you won't have the strength to maintain and strengthen your self-discipline. So keep an eye on your physical and mental well-being.

Make sure you have a healthy diet and daily rest for your mind.

Motivation is like the fuel of self-discipline. An unmotivated person becomes easy prey to despair, depression, and even anxiety, so their mental health is at risk.

Every day you must remember what drives you to continue, move forward and maintain a good rhythm of life.

You must anchor your attitude, behavior, and thoughts in an ideal, goal, achievement, or hope that awakens and keeps your motivation active. That way, you will not give in to obstacles or situations that may threaten your mood and mental health.

Self-discipline is built, and it is fed. To do this, you must value every achievement, no matter how small it may seem.

But it's not just about valuing achievements but also your efforts. Even when you think that it has not been enough, reward yourself for the effort made.

Regardless of whether the results have been as expected, you should make yourself aware of your attempt, congratulate yourself, and reward yourself because, in this way, your self-discipline will be strengthened. You will be willing to try with more discipline in the next attempt.

Self-assessment should be a constant habit in your life. Only then can you increase the level of self-discipline.

You must make a schedule that includes time to evaluate your performance, determine what you need to improve and adjust your self-discipline.

The habits we presented to you are easy to implement, and you must do them daily.

Make a schedule and include them in your day-to-day. We also recommend that you hold regular sessions with a psychologist who will guide you through creating strategies that allow you to strengthen your self-discipline.

You can always choose to go to a professional. Since these are always good options and much more professional, especially at a distance, they can help us create better self-discipline without needing to move from our homes or workplaces.

CONCLUSION

The extremes are negative; not thinking before acting can lead us to rush, while overthinking can lead us to block ourselves, which is why we must seek a healthy and flexible balance that allows us to make the most of our thinking ability. We have ideas about life, plans for the near future, and an ideal job. Probably at this point, your imagination has kicked in, and you visualize everything you want, which hasn't come true. But what to do with this? Are you waiting for the right moment to say: yes, this is exactly the time to act? Are you waiting until you have more money, find your ideal man, fix your emotional life or finish more studies? Do you know when this ideal moment will come?

It is never too late to be able to make a decision and not wait years until we dare to do something for our mental health since there is an infinity of reasons that will cause us thousands of reasons, such as anxiety, insecurity, and above all negative thoughts that will not let us rest. To our minds with thoughts like Will, I am enough? Am I good at this? But there is only one reason to take action for you: your health and emotional well-being, as well as your physical one. That is why we present you with a complete guide to follow and maintain a much healthier mental state than yesterday when you had not read this book.

Printed in Great Britain
by Amazon